COMANCHE
AND HIS CAPTAIN

To Kathy—
Best Wishes,
Janet Barrett

ALSO BY JANET BARRETT

On The Fence: A Parent's Handbook
of Horseback Riding

They Called Her Reckless
A True Story of War, Love And
One Extraordinary Horse

COMANCHE
AND HIS CAPTAIN

THE WARHORSE AND THE SOLDIER OF FORTUNE

JANET BARRETT

Tall Cedar Books
Chester, CT

First printing, 2019

Paperback ISBN 978-0-9898040-3-5

Cover and Interior Design: StoryHillCreative.com

Tall Cedar Books

36 Goose Hill Road

Chester, CT 06412

About.Comanche@gmail.com

Created with Vellum

To my husband,
Walter Terlecki,
and
To my father,
Frank Santilli.

CONTENTS

Chapter 1

SETTING COURSE

THE POPE'S EMISSARIES FANNED OUT ACROSS IRELAND AND EUROPE, from church pulpits and town squares rallying young Catholic men to join the fight for the Papal Lands. Stirring religious zeal, the envoys reminded the Irish of how Pope Pius IX had helped them during the Great Famine. England, upholder of the Anglican Church, was quick to affirm its anti-Catholic sentiments, and moved to stop the exodus by making it against the law for Irishmen to travel to Italy. The attitude of the mother country was another ugly jab at its colony, and it rankled young Myles Keogh.

In the spring of 1860, he left his home and family farm in County Carlow and answered the Pope's call. At barely 20 years old, he was a strapping six-footer with long legs, a shock of dark brown hair, and a full handlebar mustache.[1] His father had died 12 years before and Myles' older brothers, Patrick and Tom, had stepped up to take responsibility and were running the farm successfully. The servants, both live-ins and dailies, were still there, and some of his sisters lived at home with their mother. Myles had prepared for this day and he was anxious to be on his way.

For a privileged young man in mid-century Ireland it was a bold decision. Myles Keogh was the youngest son in an affluent, landowning family, by any measure an enviable position. They were not what you would call rich, nor of the upper class, but as well-established gentry, especially in Ireland, one of the poorest countries in the Western World, it was a fortunate position. Home was an estate with acres of crop fields and pastures on the outskirts of Leighlinbridge, a village of about 1,200 people on the River Barrow in the western part of the county. John and Margaret Keogh and their 12 children lived in a two-story stone farmhouse known as Orchard House. A curving driveway stretched a quarter mile from the main road to the house and, close by, various barns and sheds. Shade trees ringed the buildings and dotted the farmland beyond.[2]

The family's living quarters were laid out in the traditional style of that time, with formal and family rooms to either side of the center hallway on the main floor. Not surprisingly, the piano was in the family room which, together with the kitchen in the rear of the house, were the informal gathering places for the Keoghs and friends. The usually off-limits formal room was reserved for special visitors including the parish priest and businessmen.[3]

The Keogh family, the surname at times spelled Kehoe, had been a constant presence in County Carlow since the late 1600s. The first of the line to set down roots was Captain Thomas Kehoe, a soldier in the army of King James II of England and Ireland (also known as James VII of Scotland), the deposed Irish Catholic king. James' forces, the Jacobites, fought the Williamites, followers of the English King William III, meeting on Irish soil at the battles of the Boyne in 1690, and Aughrim in 1691. Victory went to the English and set in place many years of discrimination against Irish Catholics. With the end of fighting, much of King James' army disbanded in Limerick and Kehoe made his way 90 miles cross country and settled in Carlow in 1693, married and had a son, Patrick.[4]

Even then, Kehoe was settling in an area whose history stretched back many centuries. At Carlow, another river town on the Barrow, a megalithic tomb, said to be the graves of giants, dates back 5,000 years, its capstone the largest in Europe. Relics from the fifth century, mark the arrival of St. Patrick and the beginning of the Christian era, followed seven hundred years later by the invading Normans whose buildings turned Carlow into an important fortress. Through many centuries, the turmoil of Ireland was reflected across the whole of County Carlow, as the conflicts between populations—the native Gaelics, the Anglo-Norman and later, the Anglo-Irish Protestants—alternately simmered, erupted, and were damped down until the cycle restarted.[5]

The area Kehoe chose was, as it remains today, a rural, bucolic part of the country, dotted with small towns and farmlands. In this second smallest county in Ireland, the towns are all within a few miles of each other, many connected by the free-flowing River Barrow as it cuts north to south through the western part of the county. It is fertile land, laid out with gently rolling hills, easy to plant and harvest. Young Myles, Captain Kehoe's great great grandson, would have known the fields to be devoted to raising crops, with cattle grazed mostly for a family's personal use.

A STRONG LINK TO THE HISTORY OF IRELAND RAN THROUGH THE Kehoe family. Intertwined with their settled, comfortable existence, the Keoghs had personally felt the wrath of Great Britain, treatment that further reinforced their staunchly Catholic, anti-English commitment. A century after Captain Kehoe fought the English in what was also known as the War of the Kings, the British Army showed the level of their brutality in hanging his great grandson, Patrick. It was part of the aftermath of Carlow's part in the Rebellion of 1798, an anti-English uprising that spread across Ireland in the spring and summer of that year, aimed at eliminating England's control of Irish affairs, and ultimately achieve Ireland's independence. The organizers were the United Irishmen, a non-sectarian organization, and on the morning of May 25 they descended on Carlow Town, one of the rebels' planned points of attack. Hundreds of United Irishmen from surrounding areas surged through the streets, their numbers growing to some 1,200 as supporters joined their ranks and marched with them.

But unknown to the advancing rebels, the British Army that was garrisoned in town had been tipped off and were ready for the insurgents, thwarting their plans to take and hold key points in Carlow. Attacked as they retreated, Irish forces fared badly, with deaths of United Irishmen and civilian supporters numbering several hundred. The army, by contrast, ended the battle with less than half the manpower of the rebels and no reported casualties. In the days following, the British Army swept the area, taking into custody some 150 more who were identified or suspected of also being United Irishmen, among them Patrick Keogh. His family claims today that he was not a member,[6] but whatever efforts there were to save him then fell on deaf ears. On the morning of June 9, 1798, he was hanged in the town's main square.

The rebellion was over in Carlow, but through the summer it continued to flare up in other parts of the country. The bloodshed was grievous, figures ranging from 10,000 to 25,000 rebels and 600 British soldiers, and for all that the outcome was the opposite of what was hoped for. In 1801, the Act of Union, though opposed by many Irish, joined Ireland to Great Britain to create the United Kingdom of Great Britain and Ireland, a tighter bond than ever before.[7]

John Keogh, Myles' father, was three years old when his older brother, Patrick, died. He would have grown up knowing the story, the anguish it caused his family and the ongoing discrimination to the Irish, particularly Catholics. Whether he ever wanted to join the military we don't know, but his military allegiance would not have been to the English flag. That he was a member of the Fifth Royal Irish Lancers, as some insist he was, would have been unacceptable to him, his family says today.[8] Indeed, they scoff at the idea that anyone so anti-English ever joined a unit considered the sister to the Fifth Royal British Lancers![9] John was a gentleman farmer who wed someone who would have been thought of as a most marriageable young woman, the rich Margaret Blanchfield from County Kilkenny. As such, she would have brought a generous dowry to the marriage, a union that would have taken place around the time Orchard House was completed in 1820.

The Blanchfield lands were Rathgarvan, also known as Clifden, ten miles westward across the county line from Carlow Town. The family had settled in County Kilkenny during the Tudor period (1457 to 1603), including the titled landowner, Sir Edward Blanchfield, and his blueblood wife, Elizabeth Butler, the daughter of the second Earl of Ormond. Twice the Blanchfields experienced the indignity of the Crown confiscating their lands. The second time, in 1703, 2,903 acres were taken by King William III, who then sold off a portion. Thereafter, the Blanchfields were obliged to lease their ancestral acreage of Rathgarvan, from the Crown.[10] The family continued as the lords of Clifden Castle, built by the Norman King John about 1200 A.D. Whether or not forbearers had lived in it, by Margaret's time it was uninhabitable, albeit a cherished and historic ruin.

MYLES WALTER KEOGH WAS BORN ON MARCH 25, 1840. THE baptismal certificate listed his middle name as Tomás, likely at the insistence of the officiating priest who would have objected to Walter as a pagan name. Along with being the youngest son, he would have been one of the last born children, if not *the* last born, to John and Margaret Keogh, given that his mother was 42 at the time. Twelve offspring are commonly named in writing, but the family acknowledges a thirteenth child, Catherine, who apparently died in infancy.[11] By either count, nine grew to adulthood. Myles' siblings were brothers James, Patrick, Thomas, and John, and sisters, besides Catherine, Julia, Mary, Joanna, Bridget, Ellen, Margaret, and Fanny.

James and John died early, as did Julia, the three of them presumably of typhoid fever, a bacterial disease spread through contaminated water and food. It was a scourge of the times that claimed victims across all ages and socio-economic levels from the very poor, living in crowded, unsanitary conditions, to the rich whose contact with the bacteria was harder to pinpoint but just as deadly. Myles also contracted typhoid fever as a child but, luckier than the others, he managed to survive, nursed back to health by his sister, Margaret.[12]

What year the Keogh children died, James the eldest, and the other two, is not known, nor when Myles was taken ill. But the impact on a family, as deadly disease occurred with dreadful regularity to many in those years, cannot be denied. That four children were affected in one family, an affluent one at that, demonstrates how vicious and indiscriminate typhoid fever was in the victims it chose. Even in a large family, the norm in Ireland and elsewhere in those years, such dramatic events shifted family roles, Patrick and Thomas taking on more farm chores, and young Myles left increasingly to himself to create his own world. Two things seem to have sustained him at this time—his affinity for and love of horses and the pleasure he found in reading.

By his early twenties he was already being lauded as a superb horseman, further descriptions suggesting someone who was self confident and skilled with horses, developed from the first days the youngster sat astride a pony. Indeed, someone as brave as Keogh turned out to be, early on would have been the sort who delightedly would have urged his mount forward and galloped hell for leather across open fields.

In mid-century Ireland, as in many other countries, horses were an important part of life in rural areas. Actually, beyond walking, they were the only practical way to get around day to day. The Keoghs, at their level of financial comfort, likely had a number of them on the estate—sport horses to ride, driving horses to pull a carriage, and sturdy work horses to plow the fields. Just what breed Myles' first pony was is conjecture, of course. But choosing from one of Ireland's fine and historic breeds, that first pony could have been a Connemara or an Irish Cob.

As his legs grew longer, Myles would have retired his pony for a horse. He might have switched to an Irish Sport Horse, a bold, large-boned cross of the Irish Draught and the English Thoroughbred, a combination that preserved the elegance of the Thoroughbred and the stamina of the Draught. Or he well could have given the estate's Draught horses, a working breed also well suited to pleasure riding, a gallop now and then. But the evident abilities years later suggested a young Myles who had been more than just a rider. Stable hands tended to the horses and the overall care of the stable operation, but there is little doubt he pitched in to help, learning by doing. He pushed himself ahead, becoming a self-assured and consummate horseman. He could handle anything and was applauded for his abilities. In a few years that would bring him to an intriguing decision. The well-bred Irishman would choose as his personal mount a tough American Mustang.

DURING HIS IMPRESSIONABLE YEARS, MYLES SAW HIS DAD AS A hands-on farmer. In a country where much of the land was owned by absentee landlords who rented out small parcels of their holdings to tenant farmers, John Keogh worked his own land. He was also smart, growing as his primary crop barley for the breweries where it was always welcomed. Once harvested and bundled, it was delivered to barges waiting along the Barrow at Leighlinbridge, from there going downriver to Waterford or, via the canal system, northeast to Dublin. The good fortune to cultivate that crop would see the Keoghs through the worst devastation Ireland had ever experienced, the Great Famine.

Myles was five when the country started the downward spiral that over the next four years would reduce the population by 25 percent. Starting with slightly more than eight million people, some one million would die and another million would flee to countries near and far. The destruction began in 1845 when, depending on the part of Ireland, one-third to one-half of the potato crop failed, a catastrophe so pervasive that it was felt from the smallest villages to the largest cities. Not that Ireland was a stranger to crop failures. They had occurred with some regularity since the early 1700s, but their outbreaks were limited, affecting one part of the country or another at a time.[13] This failure was different. Even warning signs coming from Europe as, sporadically, crops failed there, were scant preparation for what would befall Ireland.

The blight, as the destructive force was commonly called, was caused by a fungus, *Phytophthora infestans*, the spores of which are thought to have originated in Mexico, jumped to the northeast United States, and from there traveled eastward on moist ocean breezes, or amongst the food stocks on clipper ships sailing in the same direction.[14] Once the fungus made landfall, it spread across Ireland with stunning speed. Report after report told of leaves on the potato plants turning black and withering, then within days the potato itself destroyed the same way.

No part of the country was immune. The devastation was everywhere, mostly because the Irish grew one type of potato, the Lumper. It was a high-yielding variety, advantageous for tenant farmers, many of whom lived on the edge, struggling to get by on the small plots of land they cultivated. Potatoes were both food for the family and the sale crop, bringing in money to pay the rent on the farmland, clothe the family, buy food to augment the potato diet, and whatever else was needed. In poor areas, potatoes were the staple crop, for the very poor their sole diet. Many of these people had no cushion, nothing extra to help in hard times. When the blight struck, the blow was swift and deadly.

Crop failures increased, in the second year wiping out three-quarters of the potatoes. With livelihoods gone people went hungry. With no money to pay the rent, harsh absentee landlords threw farmers off their lands, leaving them to scrounge or die as paupers. Charities stepped in to feed people, but it was never enough. Deaths from disease-related malnutrition and terrible hygiene and sewage conditions, as well as outright starvation grew rampant. The damage was greatest in the rural north and west of Ireland, counties Mayo and Sligo each averaging 60,000 deaths a year. Counties in the south and east, County Carlow among them, survived somewhat better, there the annual death rate averaging a sixth of the higher number.[15]

Whatever the figure, it was a devastating situation. Loss of life was compounded by an equal number of Irish citizens who, desperate yet hopeful for a better life elsewhere, emigrated to close-at-hand England, Scotland, and South Wales, and across the seas to Canada, the United States, and even as far away as Australia. Though four years after it started, the blight receded and the potato crop struggled back, the terrible repercussions to Ireland's economy, politics, and people went on for many years. Between 1846 and 1854, one and a quarter million Irish emigrated to America, and by the latter date 25 percent of all European immigrants in the U.S. were Irish.

Barley protected the Keoghs from economic loss, their brewery clients always ready to receive a shipment. But the family could not escape the emotional toll of knowing what many of their countrymen were going through, of villages affected and families wiped out. Reminders of the careless, often cruel treatment by England toward its colony were everywhere. There was ample food in country, except among the ruined farmers there was no money to buy it. As many people subsisted on bread and water, the levels of exports remained unchanged. Animals, cured meats, vegetables, fish, butter, and many other foodstuffs sailed out of Irish ports for England, igniting further hatred toward the mother country.

One can only wonder what Myles understood of what was going on. Hearing the somber, anxious tones as his parents and older siblings talked, and seeing the worry on their faces would have told him that something dire was happening. Age eight at the height of the

Famine, he would have come to understand so much more, overhearing those around him recounting in detail what people were going through. The images stayed with him and, years later, added to his resolve never to fight for England.

IN THE MIDST OF THE COUNTRY'S TURMOIL, THE KEOGHS FACED THEIR own upheaval in 1848 when John Keogh, age 53, died at Orchard House. What the cause was we don't know, nor whether it was sudden or expected. But whatever the explanation, the death of the family head can be a time of significant change, felt by everyone, each grappling with the loss in their own way as family members adjust to fill the void. Eldest son, Patrick, who would have already been working alongside his father, now stepped up to manage the estate. Tom likely helped him, while the rest of the older children, always helpful as children in large families are, now would have focused a little more attention to the care of the younger ones.

How the death of his father affected eight-year-old Myles, we can only guess. But it had to be a lonely time for him, as he experienced what would likely be one of the saddest losses he would ever know. Were they close? Did the father have a special relationship with his youngest son? What we do know is that his uncle, J.P. Blanchfield, his mother's brother, understood that his young nephew needed a friend. J.P. knew John Keogh much longer and better than Myles, and could have shared stories to help the youngster feel more connected at this disconcerting time. He stepped in to help parent Myles, the two building a friendship that lasted throughout their lives. After Myles left Ireland, when he returned for a visit he always looked forward to seeing his uncle and enjoying the conversations they would have.[16]

The same year that his father died, Myles began school. At eight he was younger than most who started that year, it being more common to tutor children at home longer before beginning school. A primary school education was free to all since the early 1830s, thanks to Ireland's National School Act, but boys and girls were taught separately. The Leighlinbridge National School, still going strong today, was known as the Boy's National School when Myles enrolled.

It had its own history, built as a chapel in 1729, then converted to a school in 1826. There, Myles Keogh showed himself to be a good student. At Orchard House, whoever tutored the youngster had found a very receptive student, as records show that upon entering school he was ahead of what was expected in first-year subjects.[17] He already knew more than the so-called basic 3Rs—written in those times as "Reading, wRiting, and aRithmetic" — and from there embraced the chance to quickly advance. He studied mathematics, geography, history, grammar, bookkeeping, and more, taught by educators eager to challenge him as he proved his ability, particularly the renown headmaster, John Conwill, who taught the senior boys.[18] One late entry on his records, "At Classics," suggests just how capable he was, the words indicative of a course of study in classical languages, namely Latin and Greek. Perhaps it was offered the same as a college preparatory course is available for a high school student to take today. It would have gone hand in hand with his love of reading, an obvious pleasure of his even before he started school. Upon admission he was already two levels ahead of the entry requirement, and by the time he graduated was at the highest level for which his teachers could award a grade.[19]

Did that passion spur Myles' interest in becoming a soldier? One can only imagine the very able young horseman seeing himself in the military-themed novels of the day. Laced with adventure and intrigue, they could have encouraged his own plans developed from family history and events in Ireland. During his school years, the very popular writings of the Anglo-Irish author, Charles Lever, would have been a ready source. Perhaps someone in the family had read a Lever novel and passed it onto Myles, or it could have come from one of Myles' classmates. Though probably not one of the books assigned by his teachers, the stories would have been afterschool favorites as copies made the rounds of the boys at school.

Lever himself was an interesting character, a practicing physician who took up writing part time to cover his gambling debts. His first foray as a writer produced a string of stories, *The Confessions of Harry Lorrequer,* that were serialized in a Dublin magazine in 1837. His work had the easy flow of a raconteur, a string of entertaining events involving hard-riding gentry and their assorted sidekicks. Many centered around military life, rich with atmosphere and panache if rather light on plot line. Lever wrote at night after his days at his medical practice and, thrilled with his quick success, said, "If this sort of thing amuses them, I can go on forever."[20] That he did, soon abandoning medicine in favor of writing full time, over the course of his life turning out more than 30 novels.

It was Charles Lever's second book, *Charles O'Malley, An Irish Dragoon*, that sources say was a favorite of young Keogh's. It, too, was serialized but a year later, in 1841, became the first of Lever's works to be published as a book. From the vantage point of later years, the protagonist, O'Malley, is an almost uncanny model for the man Myles Keogh would become. As Lever describes him at age 17, he is "tall and broad-shouldered, deadly with a gun and sure in the saddle." O'Malley's uncle lives in a ruined old castle by the River Shannon, not much of a stretch from the reality of the Keogh family and the very old Castle Clifden that still stood on the lands owned by the family of Myles' mother.

An Irish Dragoon moves through popular themes of the day, the likes of politics, fox hunting, duels and ladies fair, as the principal character, O'Malley, is drawn steadily toward his desired pursuit, finally leaving his studies for a life in the military. With an initial commission as an ensign, he heads for his first assignment, fighting on the side of Portugal against Napoleon Bonaparte in The Peninsula War (1808-1814).

Lever was prolific, producing a continuous stream of novels, usually every two to three years, with a few times just a year apart. His fans came back time and again, delighting in his many dashing heroes and the lives they led. Did Myles? To what extent did the author fire the young man's military ambitions? To what extent and when did Myles come to his own decisions? Was Lever's writing icing on the cake to a young man who already felt a wanderlust and understood where his allegiance lay? At the very least, they were of a common mind. More than that is conjecture, but the similarities between Lever's O'Malley and Keogh are intriguing.

Beyond O'Malley, Myles might well have been stirred in those early years by a poem that spread like wildfire during the Crimean War. It was *The Charge of the Light Brigade,* written by Britain's poet laureate, Alfred, Lord Tennyson, six weeks after a suicidal charge by the British light cavalry at the Battle of Balaclava in October 1854.

The order to charge the enemy was in error, although at exactly what point communication failed is still debated. Nevertheless, 673 horsemen galloped headlong into the blazing Russian artillery, the terrible outcome of which was 278 soldiers killed or wounded and 335 horses killed. Despite that, Tennyson chose to glorify the valor of the cavalry and the heroics of common soldiers versus the high command.[21] The appreciation spread throughout the British Empire as newspapers printed the poem, soldiers at the front received copies, and for decades to come, school children studiously memorized and recited the many stanzas.

As it is said, that a poem committed to memory lives within the person forever, this author can attest to that in her grandfather, an Englishman from Manchester, England by way of Toronto, Canada. As an old man, he could still recite Tennyson's ode. I was very young and had no idea what he was talking about but, thinking back, I remember the jaunty cadence that spoke of galloping horses and riders at the ready, as it began:

Half a league half a league

Half a league onward,
All in the valley of Death
Rode the six hundred

and ended…

Honour the charge they made!
Honour the Light Brigade,
Noble six hundred!

Perhaps a 14-year-old Irish schoolboy was old enough to understand the serious intent, and the glorification of bravery, honor and valor. The poem did not glorify war per se, but to a young man it certainly could capture the excitement of warfare.

AT A TIME WHEN A COLLEGE EDUCATION WAS GENERALLY RESERVED for members of the socially prominent, Protestant upper class, a smart, focused, and mature Myles Keogh enrolled at St. Patrick's College, then one of Ireland's foremost boarding schools, in neighboring Carlow Town. Formerly known as Carlow College—St. Patrick's, it is one of Ireland's oldest Catholic colleges, accepting its first students in October 1793. Myles was young, possibly not yet age 15, but apparently ready for the challenge.

His college years are void of details, nothing about his interests, his courses of study, or anything else is noted from that time. The only thing we know is that Myles left St. Patrick's before completing his studies, there being no record of his graduation. His family's best guess is that he left in the spring of 1858 and took a job at a local bank, a branch of the Royal Bank of Ireland in Bagenalstown, seven miles from home.[23] Had he become impatient with formal learning? Was it time to move on, to start life as he foresaw it? As the third son in the Keogh family, there would have been no role for him in running the estate, that being well in hand by his elder brothers and the hired help. Was the bank a place to bide his time and set aside some money as he planned his next move? After all, how long was he to stay in a staid, rigidly controlled world of pounds and pence?

What we do know is that two years later Myles Keogh took that first important step. Following the tradition of countrymen over hundreds of years, he left Ireland to fight another man's war. He would become a soldier of fortune. What dreams was he fulfilling, what honor was he upholding as he set out for foreign shores? Italy was a good place to start finding out.

Chapter 2

THE POPE CALLS

THE BISHOPS HAD SOLD THEIR MESSAGE WELL. FROM IRELAND AND countries across Europe 18,000 men left farms and towns, homes, families, and jobs, and headed for Italy. Included were 1,400 Irishmen. Many saw it as their turn to help Pope Pius IX after what he had done for them. At the height of the Great Famine, his Holiness had issued a papal encyclical asking Catholics around the world to open their hearts and give to aid victims, then underscored his position by giving one thousand Roman coins from his own pocket to encourage such help.[1] Now, as the bishops asked for a quid pro quo, they also pointed to England's long-standing ill treatment of the Irish. To fight someone elsewhere, the emissaries told audiences, would serve them well when the time came to liberate their own country.[2]

By mid-19th century, Pius IX's political position was threatened. The Italians, while they savored their regional individualities as Romans, Florentines, Milanese, Sicilians, Neapolitans and so forth, were ready to unify. The patchwork of independent kingdoms and duchies, variously aligned with neighboring countries, was changing. Among the many entities, the land ruled by the Pope was seen as a reflection of his earthly power. It was a huge swath of territory that stretched like a wide belt across Italy's midsection from coast to coast, and included today's regions of Umbria, Lazio, Marche, and parts of Emilia-Romagna.[3] If the area was absorbed by *Risorgimento*, as the movement toward unification was called, Pius IX feared the loss would also reduce his spiritual power. Who he was to the world—His Holiness, Head of the Catholic Church—was his only defense. He had no standing army, and he hoped the men who were arriving would be a force sufficient to save his lands from being absorbed into this newly forming Italian nation. True, Italians were staunch Catholics, but they were far more swept up with the idea of Italy becoming one country than they were with the concerns of their Pope.

England's opposition to the Pope was long standing, but events in the spring of 1860 tested the depth of that position. The bishops had not only raised a Papal army but funds to support it. Irish parishioners alone donated 80,000 pounds, more than $12 million in today's money, to the cause. Now, when young men embarked for Italy, either alone or in groups, the British government took notice and attempted to stop them. An old law, the Foreign Enlistment Act of 1819, originally designed to preserve the neutrality of Great Britain by prohibiting its subjects from fighting for a foreign power, was resurrected to stem the exodus. Going to fight for the Pope was illegal, and those who did it broke the law.[4]

A commonplace trip had suddenly become complicated. But to the advantage of the Irish, loopholes in the law made it difficult to enforce. There were two so-called pass-throughs, situations the authorities would not question. Young men traveling in a group, in the company of a priest who vouched for them as being on a pilgrimage, was one such scenario. A number of men, all identifying themselves as workmen, yet still traveling with a priest, was another way. Even though authorities knew that many groups heading for Europe that spring were ignoring the law and would wind up in Italy, anti-Catholic attitudes in general were enough of a tinderbox without questioning the intent of a priest and his charges.

. . .

MYLES KEOGH WOULD HAVE GONE BY BUGGY THE EIGHT MILES TO THE nearest train station, that being at Carlow Town, taken there by someone at Orchard House or a buggy service in Leighlinbridge. Train service was quite good in Ireland by then, especially in the south, including the station at Carlow that opened in 1846.[5] From there he likely headed north to connect with the main Dublin-Limerick railroad line, but beyond that we can't be sure how he made his way. Whoever his travel companions, they were not just from County Carlow, judging by two friends he made early on from the southern seaside counties of Cork and Waterford. Joseph O'Keefe, a year younger than Myles, was a nephew of the Bishop of Cork, and Daniel Kiely, the eldest at 30, was from Waterford, the two and Keogh forming a close friendship that would endure for years to come.

Itineraries were various, groups having a choice of many ports from which to sail, and once in Europe, how they made their way to Italy was equally imaginative. The sum of it, of course, was frustrating if not downright infuriating to the British government. Judging by passenger lists throughout the 19th century, ships left from ports on all sides of Ireland, most often Queenstown in Cork and Waterford, both in the south, Dublin in the east, Limerick and Galway in the west, and Newery, Belfast, Londonderry, and Sligo in the north.

The first mentioned, Queenstown (formerly Cobh), on Grand Island in Cork Harbor, was a major transatlantic port and the most frequently used by travelers in general. It was named in 1849 to commemorate Queen Victoria's visit to Ireland that year, the same year the Potato Famine abated. In the wake of that horror, it was the point of departure for many Irish emigrants leaving their homeland, the last port of call on their way to a new life. Darkly, it was also the final stop for the RMS Titanic before it started across the Atlantic Ocean and, three days later, hit an iceberg and sank. With it went 79 of the 123 people who had boarded at Queenstown. In 1922 the name was changed back to the port's original, Cobh.

As their ships set sail from Ireland, most of the groups heading to Italy had grown to between 20 and 40 men. Some took the shorter sea route, sailing to Le Havre on France's North Atlantic coast and traveling from there, by rail and coach, through Belgium and Austria to Italy. Others went south on an all-sea route, landing first at Marseilles and from there sailing to Rome. One of the largest groups set out from Limerick, some 75 men coming from surrounding areas and many occupations—laborers, shopkeepers, doctors, lawyers, farmers, bankers, even members of the Cork police department. For the trip, they listed themselves as harvesters, traveling first by train to Waterford, from there by ship to Wales, then again by train to London. The final leg, by sea, brought them to Ostend, Belgium. The send-off for the Limerick group, as for others, were the crowds that cheered as they marched through the streets of Limerick, then welcomed them as they traveled through Europe, in Austria and elsewhere enthusiastically meeting them at train stops, bringing flowers, religious objects, food and wine.[6]

Did the Pope's entreaties give Keogh the opening he had been looking for? Intelligent as he was, and well prepared for college study by headmaster Conwill of the National School, studies at the renowned St. Peter's College could not hold his interest. It was not a question of finances as his family had paid for his education.[7] Whether he left in the spring of senior year or more likely, as his family suggests, two years earlier, Myles Keogh was searching for something else. Looking back at the fast pace of the next few years, soldiering was in his blood. Even more, did he have a sense of his own strengths and how capable, indeed what an exceptional military man he would become?

This first time, Keogh's initial battle in Italy, as in the other engagements that followed, he would fight as an Irishman, not as a British subject, and not for the English flag. It was in the spirit of what the Irish had done centuries before, those called the Wild Geese, who had gone to France, the Netherlands, Spain and elsewhere to fight on the side of the host country. Myles' great-great-grandfather, Captain Kehoe, could have been one, but he chose to stay in Ireland and settle down.

Many of Captain Kehoe's comrades, the defeated Jacobites who put down their arms in Limerick at the end of the War of the Kings, would board ships with their commander, Patrick Sarsfield, and sail for France. These forces of the deposed King James II, beaten at the Boyne and Aughrim, withstood final capitulation in the Siege of Limerick until late September 1691. The Treaty of Limerick, signed by Sarsfield on October 3, 1691, gave permission for him to lead a fighting force of some 14,000 Irishmen to France where they joined regiments that had gone the year before. Many took with them their wives and children. In addition to safe passage for those leaving, Sarsfield believed that the treaty guaranteed the rights of Irish Catholics remaining in their homeland. But the British quickly reneged and instituted the harshly discriminatory Penal Laws that, over the next two hundred years, would be the basis for stripping the Irish of their lands, persecuting them for their religion, and taking away their rights of citizenship.[8]

The betrayal set the stage for a century of Irishmen fighting and dying for France. Some fought for adventure, some fought to make a living, but many more to avenge their enemy, England. It is estimated that in that period a half million Irishmen or more gave their lives in service to France. Soldiers would come home between insurrections to replenish their ranks. Then, departing again on ships that had smuggled in brandy and wine, they would be listed on the outbound manifest as "wild geese."

The fighting prowess of these warriors turned the tide for France against England at the Battle of Fontenoy in 1745, during the War for

Austrian Succession. That contribution would also be the high point for them as defenders of French interests, though their presence continued as part of that country's military until late in the 18th century. England's King George II, acknowledging the Irish prowess after Fontenoy, said, "Cursed be the laws which deprive me of such subjects," a comment that rang true again and again.[9] Irish battalions made their mark in many of the armies of Europe, including Spain, Austria, Russia, and Sweden, some fighting in wars before their mass exodus from Ireland in 1691, many thereafter. They also crossed the seas to fight in Chile and Argentina, with the French at Savannah, Georgia and elsewhere in the American Revolution, and with both the Union and Confederate troops in the American Civil War.

WHAT AN INSPIRING SEND-OFF IT WAS FOR MYLES AND THE OTHER young men leaving Ireland to fight for the Pope. The spirit of the Wild Geese was alive again, and by their actions these soldiers were upholding a noble heritage. The bishops who recruited them had promised that they would all fight together as Irishmen had done before, one powerful force to be called the Battalion of St. Patrick.[10] Further, they were to be properly trained, wear new green uniforms designed especially for them, and be paid a livable wage for their efforts.

But reality did not match the promises. Training, hurriedly begun in late June 1860, when volunteers from ten countries gathered in Rome, was complicated for the Irish as English was not one of the languages used by the Papal Army. The Irish were clothed in a haphazard mix of new and used Austrian uniforms from previous wars, the promised green uniforms, the signature of who they were, never materializing. Their weapons were not up to par, pay turned out to be paltry and mostly reabsorbed by day-to-day expenses and, perhaps most disappointing, they never fought as one unit but were split into companies and sent to defend separate areas within the

Papal States.[11] Some couple hundred young men went back to Ireland, disgusted to the point of no longer wanting to participate. But most men moved beyond their grievances to fight with distinction. As the anticipated battles loomed closer, Keogh and his friends, Joseph O'Keefe and Daniel Kiely, positioned themselves well, each securing the rank of second lieutenant in the Papal Army. The war would be short, but pivotal in the drive to unify Italy. It would also change the lives of three friends.

By 1860, *Risorgimento* had come very close to achieving its objectives. With the Second Italian War of Independence, also known as the Franco-Austrian War, in 1859, Austria gave up the region of Lombardy and its capital, Milan, thereby bringing almost all of northern Italy under the Kingdom of Piedmont-Sardinia. The following year, in the central Italian duchies of Parma, Tuscany, and Modena, people voted for unification. What remained were the Kingdom of the Two Sicilies, that also joined in 1860, and the region of Veneto and its capital, Venice, which Austria held for another six years.

There was one more holdout—and those were the Papal States. They had been in the hands of the Papacy since the eighth century A.D., and now their days of independence were numbered. As the forces of unification were squeezing his lands from both the north and south, Pius IX's Papal Army readied for a fight. Two leaders orchestrated the opposition—the revolutionary, Giuseppe Garibaldi, and the statesman-diplomat, Camillo Benso, Count of Cavour. However, they were of opposite minds as to the government they sought. Garibaldi encouraged rebellion with the ultimate goal of Italy as a republic. Cavour, a monarchist, worked to unite the various parts as the Kingdom of Italy under King Vittorio Emmanuel II, then the king of Piedmont-Sardinia. Both would achieve their dream, Cavour first when northern and southern Italy became the Kingdom of Italy in 1861, though parts of the final map were still to be added. Eighty-five years later, in 1946, Garibaldi's vision became reality when the Italian people voted to become the Italian Republic.

Piedmontese troops moved against the Papal States in September 1860, their intent two-fold: to take over the region, and then to continue south and join up with Garibaldi's forces moving north. Garibaldi had taken Sicily and was poised to move to the mainland and attack Naples. The invasion was backed by the British Navy, another reflection of Britain's support of unification and opposition to the Irish fighting on behalf of the Pope. With Naples' defeat, the Kingdom of the Two Sicilies was united with the rest of Italy. The first goal, taking the Papal lands, was achieved in eighteen days and four battles. At its conclusion, the Pope had lost all his holdings except Rome and a small area surrounding it.

Papal troops had trained since mid-summer, and if they were not supplied with appropriate equipment, they were mentally ready for what they expected lay ahead. Their commander, the highly regarded French general, Christophe Léon Louis Juchault de Lamoricière, preemptively positioned troops at key points within the Papal States including Perugia, due north of Rome, and the port of Ancona to the east on the Adriatic coast. Piedmontese forces outnumbered the Papal Army almost two to one, 35,000 of the enemy crossing into the region on September 11th.[12] Fighting through the month of September 1860, they attacked first at Perugia on September 13th, then Spoleto on the 17th, Castelfidardo on the 18th, and finally Ancona, which remained under siege from the 18th until the 29th. Added to their power in numbers, the enemy was better trained, better outfitted and better equipped than the Papal troops. The latter fought valiantly but ultimately lost all four battles. Even so, the ability of the Irish stood out, other members of the multi-national force remembering them as tough, stand-their-ground fighters.

The clash of forces at Perugia was a disheartening first engagement for the Papal Army. The single company (143 soldiers and two officers)[13] that went up against the invading Piedmontese, engaged them in running fights through the narrow streets of the city. A band of Irish among them finally took an abandoned building from where they fought fiercely until enemy numbers and their artillery forced the Irish to surrender.[14]

Four days later, the battle at Spoleto was quite different, with Papal forces holding their ground far longer before accepting defeat. Better than four times as many fighters as were at Perugia, half of them Irish and the other half of mixed nationalities,[15] went up against 2,500 of the enemy. Even with reduced strength, Papal troops protected key points of the famed Castle Albornozian for 14 hours, fighting the enemy hand-to-hand despite continuing pounding from their field artillery.[16]

Without a break, the largest engagement of the war broke out the next day, September 18th, at Castelfidardo, a city 14 miles south of Ancona but inland from the coast. General Lamoricière was moving most of the Papal troops to Ancona, to fortify that port city, when their way was blocked by General Enrico Cialdini, commander of the Piedmontese Army, and his Fourth Army Corps. Lamoricière was forced to engage in battle, his Irish forces again being noted for toughness and bravery beyond that of other Papal soldiers.

As one Belgian soldier described them in a letter to his family, Irish troops fighting in a field rushed forward to retrieve guns abandoned by the retreating enemy. The Italians and Swiss, he said, backed off. But the Irish, joined by French and Belgian troops stormed ahead, "like lions." An Irish company, he added, "smashed three companies of the enemy in pieces."[17]

Ultimately, however, such bravura could not save the day. Papal forces, badly weakened, eventually surrendered. After Castelfidardo the Papal Army, whose men initially numbered 18,000 strong, through casualties and others taken prisoner, at this point was reduced by three-quarters. What remained was a force of just over 4,600 troops garrisoned at Ancona since July.[18] Lamoricière had pre-positioned Papal troops there before fighting commenced, anticipating that Piedmontese troops would want to use the port, a major one on the Adriatic Sea. Now he desperately hoped that if he could hold the port long enough, other countries would step up to defend the Pope.

Castelfidardo did not end as General Lamoricière had planned. He had given the order for the Ancona garrison to join the battle, an order that by error was never carried out.[19] Those thousands of men never left the port. As Castelfidardo fell into enemy hands, Lamoricière and 45 of his men managed to escape and make their way to Ancona.[20] General Cialdini, according to his battle report, assumed that the retreating band was the tail end of the garrison that had rushed back to defend the port. Presumably, spies had told the Piedmontese commander that the full force was on its way, and in the fog of battle no one ever knew what had actually happened.[21]

KEOGH FOUGHT AT ANCONA, A SECOND LIEUTENANT IN ONE OF THE four companies (in all 440 soldiers and 16 officers) of the Irish Battalion engaged in that final battle.[22] Whether he was part of the force garrisoned at the port all along—likely chafing at his inability to join the fight elsewhere—or if, indeed, he saw action elsewhere, is unclear. As an officer, it is possible that he saw combat at Castelfidardo, and was one of the small group that mounted up and made the dash to Ancona with Lamoricière. Either way, the truth of his presence at Ancona is embodied in the *Cross of the Order of St. Gregory the Great*, an honor specifically commemorating his gallantry in combat at the port city, given to him by Pope Pius IX. The elegant eight-point cross suspended on a red and gold ribbon, still awarded today, signifies service above and beyond the expected. Since established by Pope Gregory XVI in 1831, it has honored individuals who have made significant contributions in the military, government, philanthropy, the arts, and other fields.

Ancona's garrison proved tenacious in holding the port for 11 days. At one point toward the end of the siege, the Irish were remembered for turning a retreat into a fierce bayonet fight.[23] Was Keogh one of those showing his fighting prowess as he wielded his weapon? Or was it another time that his bravery was apparent? While we cannot know exactly when it was that his superiors saw a performance noteworthy enough to tell the Pope, we know that the *Order of St. Gregory the Great* spoke to a specific time or times when Keogh's actions stood out above his peers. That trait in Keogh, to push himself to greater contribution, would occur again and again in the years to follow.

On day ten, even as Papal forces tenaciously held the enemy at bay, 13 warships from the Sardinian navy appeared in the harbor and commenced a relentless bombardment, turning their cannons on the Citadel at water's edge. Overpowered and with no prospects of reinforcements, Papal troops could no longer hold on. The next day, Ancona fell, Papal soldiers raising the white flag. Inexplicably, the enemy bombed the port one more time, then accepted General Lamoricière's surrender.[24] On September 29, 1860 the Papal War was over. Among all troops, it is thought that between 70 and 100 Irishmen were killed or wounded.[25]

For General Lamoricière, the defeat of Ancona was a severe blow at the end of a long and illustrious military career, one that had followed a family tradition of army service for generations. He served in Africa for 17 years, subduing Arabs in battle while building detente between the French and Algerians. He also briefly served as the country's Minister of War, and for a few years was involved in politics. After the Papal defeat, he retired to his chateaux in west-central France and spent his final years engaged in good works for the Catholic Church including building a church for the poor parish of Louroux-Beconnais, generously supporting an orphanage, and founding a Catholic school. As an accolade, the French people collected money for a sword of honor but he would not take it, calling himself a defeated general. The Pope, however, would not take such an answer and presented Lamoricière with the *Cross of the Order of Christ,* the only honor he would accept.[26]

THREE DAYS AFTER ANCONA FELL, ALL IRISH TROOPS WERE SENT TO Genoa as prisoners of war. Officers, Keogh among them, boarded the ship *Count Cavour* and sailed around the boot of Italy to the Mediterranean port. The rank-and-file made the trip overland, shorter by miles but not as comfortably. Incarceration lasted three weeks, reports of the treatment ranging from acceptable to terrible, likely enlisted men getting the worst of it. Negative reports described the food as meager and clothes supposedly sent from the Pope but never delivered.[27] For the officers, however, prison seemed more like detention. They were allowed to go into the nearest town in the evening, bound only by their honor to return to the barracks, presumably by the next morning.

Irish troops were released in late October and most began the journey back to Ireland. Beginning on October 20, the Papal ship *Byzantine* ferried men along the Mediterranean to Marseilles. From there it was overland to Paris, and then onto Le Havre, where the paddle steamer, *Dee*, packed with more than 900 Irishmen, headed for Queenstown. As they moved into the harbor at Cork on November 3, 1860, crowds on shore cheered and two steamers sailed to meet them. Onboard were a welcoming committee, two bands, 1,000 new wool suits from the local tailors, and a like number of prepared breakfasts. Celebrations continued through the day, concluding with crowds waving the men off as they boarded trains for homes across Ireland and more festivities to come.[28]

Post combat, each man who fought for the Pope was awarded the *Medaglia Pro Petri Sede.* The wording, on the medal's face, translates to "For the seat of Peter," thus The Vatican. On the reverse side, also in Latin, it says, "The victory of our flock conquers the world with our faith." The Vatican declared the many thousands who served in the war as "meritorious of the Catholic Church, the Holy See and all human society."[29] It was an eloquent thank you to all who had put their day-to-day lives on hold to come and fight for the Pope. Thereafter, formal photographs showed Keogh proudly wearing both the *Medaglia Pro Petri Sede* and the *Cross of the Order of St. Gregory the Great* on his left chest. Years later, one would serve as a talisman like no other.

MYLES KEOGH WAS NOT ONBOARD THE *DEE*. HE DID NOT GO HOME. Instead, he had gone to Rome, one of 45 Papal soldiers who had been invited by Pope Pius IX to join the newly organized Papal Guard, a select and greatly reduced version of the Papal Army. It was a way to keep the essence of the Pope's army alive, even if barely a fraction of what it had been. Within the Guard, the Irish soldiers were given their own battalion, the Company of St. Patrick.[30] Thirteen officers were needed and Keogh, along with his friends O'Keefe and Kiely, again positioned themselves well. Each of them accepted a commission, Keogh and O'Keefe as second lieutenants and Kiely as a first lieutenant.

To be invited to join such an elite group was a high compliment. Many would have coveted such a plum assignment. Whatever his private thoughts about his future direction, as a Catholic, Keogh among the others would have appreciated the honor of continuing to serve the Pope. The problem was that it was a ceremonial post without action or challenge, the comfortable life and dashing uniform it afforded of little appeal. In short order Myles Keogh was bored. Now close to the heart of Papal power, he found himself disenchanted with the politics and deceits therein, something he wrote as much to his family.[30] For him to remain a member of the Papal Guard, even within the small and select Company of St. Patrick, was simply a poor fit.

The Papal Guard and its Irish contingent did not last long, anyway. In September 1862, less than two years after it was formed, the Irish unit was disbanded and the remainder of the Guard absorbed by the Papal Zouaves (a name stemming from a French-Belgian group in the Papal War). That group remained to defend the Pope until his last stronghold, Rome, was defeated and Italy was unified in 1870. But Myles Keogh was gone, even before the demise of the Guard. Tempted by new challenges, he had resigned his commission in Rome. The Papal War had ended much too soon for the young soldier of fortune, and he was ready for his next assignment. The Americans came calling at exactly the right time.

In 1862 the American Civil War was a year old and in the north the Union Army was running short of officers. The tradition of a military career was more ingrained in the South than in the North, and once the South seceded from the Union, the greater supply of trained military, especially officers, went with it. After a year, the North felt the shortage and looked to ways to rebuild its ranks. With the Papal War ended, the Pope's former soldiers were a source to be pursued. High-placed Americans, noted individuals from various walks of life, headed to Rome and Ireland to persuade them of the Union forces' pressing need. Among them were the Irish-born archbishops John Hughes of the Archdiocese of New York, and John Purcell of the Archdiocese of Cincinnati. Both were advisors to William H. Seward, former governor of New York and now President Lincoln's Secretary of State, who was orchestrating the foreign recruitment. In Italy, they found three ready recruits in Keogh, Kiely, and O'Keefe. All of them, ready to move forward, signed on for their next war.

Margaret Keogh, age 64, had died in early 1862 at Orchard House, and from Italy her son went home briefly to pay his respects. Given his close connection to his uncle, J.P. Blanchfield, he surely would have found time to visit with him and, as likely, took a good look at the place he would not see again in the same light. Several years passed before he returned, from then on a visitor to his homeland.

KEOGH AND KIELY (O'KEEFE TRAVELED SEPARATELY) BOOKED passage on the passenger liner, *Kangaroo,* of the Liverpool, New York and Philadelphia Steamship Company. The company, nicknamed the "Inman Line" for its founder and owner, William Inman, was one of the foremost passenger ship lines of the second half of the 19th century. The *Kangaroo* had been a troop transport during the Crimean War, and thereafter joined several other Inman ships in providing weekly transatlantic crossings between Liverpool and the Port of New York with a stop at Queensland, a feature added in 1859.[31]

On this voyage, the ship left Liverpool on Wednesday, March 19, 1862, but it makes little sense that Keogh and Kiely backtracked across the Irish Sea to board there. In all likelihood, Myles joined his friend at the latter's home in County Waterford, or in Cork, and the two boarded the *Kangaroo* at Queensland, traveling first class. The fare was $80.00 from either starting point to New York, payable in gold or equivalent currency, all this according to an 1863 poster promoting the Inman line.[32]

The *Kangaroo* steamed into Lower New York Bay on Tuesday, April 1. From there, heading into Upper New York Bay it dropped anchor to await the formalities of arrival. An immigration officer, sailing out from the tip of Manhattan Island, went aboard to assess the condition of the ship and its passengers, the numbers in first, second and steerage classes, who was sick, and if any had died. Once it passed muster, the *Kangaroo* moved closer to shore, passengers were transferred to barges and tugboats for the last short hop to land, and the liner turned into the East River to berth in one of the slips along the South Street Seaport.

Facing the new arrivals as they stepped ashore was a round stone fort, originally built to defend New York harbor against the British in the early 1800s. It was an island in the bay then named Castle Clinton in honor of New York's governor at the time, DeWitt Clinton. But as foreign threats evaporated, landfill joined the fort to Manhattan and, renamed as the more inviting Castle Garden, became a beer garden, then a grand music hall. In 1855, the venue took on a very different role, this time as the Emigrant Landing Depot, New York's first processing center for travelers from other countries to the U.S., the primary concern then the health of those arriving.

Once in the Garden, travelers claimed their baggage that had been offloaded separately from the *Kangaroo,* and availed themselves of other services. Depot staff provided travel information and sold tickets to destinations beyond New York—for Keogh and Kiely, train tickets to Washington, D.C.—and a money exchange was said to offer the best rate available when the newcomers swapped their native currency for U.S. dollars.

The welcome to New York could be tumultuous, a single liner carrying several hundred passengers, all of who crowded into Castle Garden at the same time. Some people had family waiting, many more were on their own, trying to figure out where to go next. Some spoke English, many more spoke other languages, the air filled with a jumble of foreign tongues. In time, the way Eastern European immigrants pronounced Castle Garden—*Kesselgarden*—morphed into Yiddish slang for a noisy, chaotic space.[33]

The clamor continued once travelers had cleared the Garden and found themselves outside the stone walls. Here every imaginable vendor from legitimate to con artist were waiting to work the crowds, offering their services and plying their trades. There were military recruiters for the Union Army, charities providing food and clothing, rooming house operators renting lodging, to the other extreme of the worst sharpies and scalpers one could imagine.

As they made their way through the throng, Keogh and Kiely had an itinerary and a plan before them that likely included a few days' stay in New York before proceeding on their way. Climbing into one of the horse and buggies waiting outside the Garden, they headed uptown into the hub of the biggest city either had ever visited. New York's population in 1862, by then well over 815,000, was far larger than other cities they knew such as Dublin, Rome, likely London and maybe even Paris.

Still, New York of that time took up a small portion of the city it would become. The majority of the population lived, worked, and enjoyed their leisure activities below today's 42nd Street on Manhattan Island. The rich were escaping the crowded conditions by pushing north and building their grand mansions on upper Fifth Avenue, but working class New Yorkers, already complaining about a crowded city with traffic jams and rising rents, sounded very much as they do today.

The newspaper editor, Asa Green, writing 25 years before Keogh arrived, fumed at "omnibuses, coaches, and other vehicles" for the difficulties in getting across Broadway, a thorough with no organization to its traffic flow:

> To perform the feat with any degree of safety, you must button your coat tight about you, see that your shoes are secure at the heels, settle your hat firmly on your head, look up street and down street, at the self-same moment, to see what carts and carriages are upon you, and then run for your life.[34]

As to the high cost of living, the red flags were up with Green warning that the increases would bring "such discouragements and obstacles to the dwellers of New York that they will naturally turn their backs upon the city and seek a residence elsewhere...".[35]

Yet, the population continued to grow, and with it the city's vitality as restaurants, shops, hotels, and places of entertainment multiplied to serve residents and visitors alike. Where the three friends stayed, dined, and otherwise spent their time, we have no way of knowing. But it would be surprising if the same young men who crossed the Atlantic Ocean as first class passengers would not have treated themselves well, staying at one of the better hotels like the Astor House, its competitor the St. Nicholas Hotel, or perhaps the Fifth Avenue Hotel, and dining at New York's nicer restaurants. They may have even done a little shopping in the country's oldest department store, Lord & Taylor, or its new competitor, R.H. Macy & Co., and spent an evening at the theater, the opera, or the symphony.

Whatever their choices, it likely crossed their minds that they should enjoy themselves. They knew they might never pass this way again, that being the nature of where they were going.

Chapter 3

THE UNION CAUSE

MYLES KEOGH, DANIEL KIELY, AND JOSEPH O'KEEFE ARRIVED AT Washington's Baltimore and Ohio Depot among throngs of recruits that daily poured off trains from the north, soon to head south to the battlefields.[1] The trip had started early that day at the foot of Cortlandt Street in lower Manhattan, where a ferry took on passengers for the short hop across the Hudson River to the New Jersey shore. Railroad travel was well established in the northeast and mid-Atlantic states by 1862, but the bridges and tunnels that would allow trains to cross rivers uninterrupted were still to come. For the time being, ferries bridged the gap.

Directly across the river in New Jersey were several passenger terminals, each built for a separate train line. The Baltimore and Ohio (B&O) by then was the largest and best established of the railroad companies, offering service from New York through to Washington. Once outside the depot, the three found themselves in the heart of the city, at the intersection of New Jersey Avenue and C Street, just south of the U.S. Capitol building. The capitol dome, under construction and wrapped in scaffolding, was a very visible landmark for visitors.[2]

In the spring of 1862, with the Civil War entering its second year, Washington, D.C. was a city on heightened war footing. Situated across the Potomac River from the Confederate state of Virginia to the west and the Border State of Maryland to the east, the heartbeat of the Union was a sought after conquest of the enemy. Likewise, if Union troops could take Richmond, Virginia, the Confederate capitol, it would paralyze southern efforts to continue the war.

Only a few years before, Washington, D.C. had been a small, quiet city. Much of its population, about 75,000 by 1860, still left town each summer to escape the blistering heat. But within two years, it was a very different place. Not only did troops pile into the city before moving out to fight the war, but exhausted troops came back to repair and rebuild their ranks and go out again.

A multitude of construction projects were underway, changing the face of Washington as the Federal government expanded to direct the war and prepare for its aftermath. A defensive perimeter had gone up around Washington, protecting the city against possible Confederate attacks.

The elaborate system was a 37-mile ring of fortifications around the Capitol that included 68 forts, gun batteries, rifle pits, in all emplacements for 1,500 weapons.[3] Numerous hospitals were constructed to care for the growing number of sick and injured brought in from the war zones. The same institutions also grappled with patients felled by diseases spreading within the city's swelling population.

EVEN AS KEOGH AND HIS FRIENDS ABSORBED THE SCENE AROUND them and contemplated what was likely ahead, a few days in Washington were an exhilarating prospect. The intent of the trip was clear, to finalize an arrangement set in motion in Rome, that they would join Union forces fighting in the Civil War. But the stay in Washington,

D.C., a city Myles Keogh would come to know over many trips in the following years, was an experience in and of itself beginning with where they stayed.

They took rooms at one of the city's grand old hotels, like many beginning years before as a single boardinghouse or tavern. Neighboring townhouses were added until the owner had acquired a string of lodgings on the street, fancied up the whole with a facade, added a roofline and a main entrance and, finally, an important-sounding name. John Davis did it first, opening Davis' Hotel in 1805.[4]

Its next owner, Jesse Brown, purchased the building in 1820, hung an enticing painting of Pocahontas out front and renamed the hotel, Brown's Indian Queen Hotel. A noted showman of his time, he pampered his guests right up to the grand gesture of placing full decanters of brandy and whiskey on every table in the dining room.[5] Whether the generous libations continued is not known but Brown's sons, following their father's death, gave the hotel the élan of a marble facade and named it Brown's Marble Hotel. That was the version Keogh and his two friends enjoyed.

From its start, as Davis' Hotel, the establishment was a magnet for historical events, first as the site of James Madison's second inaugural ball in 1813, then both of James Monroe's inaugurals in 1817 and 1821. Under Brown's tenure, John Tyler was sworn in as president in 1841, after the untimely death of President William Henry Harrison, one month after he had taken office.[6]

Yet, even with its colorful past, it was the hotel's next incarnation and name change that people remember. Three years after Keogh and his friends stayed there, it changed hands again and was renamed the Metropolitan. The name lasted the rest of its days until the Metropolitan closed in 1932. By way of a remembrance the following year, the *Washington Post* noted that it "had been in continuous operation longer than any other hotel in America." Two years later, the building was torn down to disappear in a pile of rubble.[7]

Knowledge of the young men's backgrounds, particularly their service in the Papal War and the fact that they were about to join the Union army, must have made its way around Brown's Marble Hotel. Within short order, Keogh and Kiely were approached by an inventor and became instant experts on a piece of military equipment.

The entrepreneur, Horace Day, a manufacturer and pioneer in the processing of rubber, was seeking endorsements for a poncho tent he had invented. Presumably a hybrid of a rain covering and a shelter, it could protect the upright individual, then be stretched out and secured to the ground, to cover someone while sitting or lying down.

Keogh and Kiely obliged with enthusiastic reviews plus agreed that their names could be used by Day in an advertisement in one of the Washington newspapers.[8] Whether the exchange and publicity generated any interest or, even more, if Day sent the two to the battlefield with a sample tent, was never reported. But with their own prior experiences, the two young men were comfortable enough to step up and offer Day their opinions.

Within days the three had arranged a meeting with William Henry Seward, President Lincoln's Secretary of State, to move forward the process of their induction into the army. Seward had vied with Lincoln to be the Republican party's standard bearer in the 1860 election. But once the nomination and then the presidency went to Lincoln, he was happy to have Seward in his cabinet.

The meeting was not a cold call as each carried letters of introduction to the secretary that had been to given to them in Italy. At the same time, Archbishop Hughes had written directly to Seward, touting the men's qualifications. He, in turn, wrote Secretary of War Edwin Stanton on their behalf:

Department of State
Washington, 4th April 1862

To the Honorable E.M. Stanton

Secretary of War

Sir:

I am informed by Archbishop Hughes of New York who is now at Rome, that he has written to you in behalf of Messrs Kiely and Keogh, two gentlemen recently officers of the Papal army, who are desirous of being appointed in the military service of the United States. As this wish on their part is understood to be favored by Cardinal Antonelli and by the Pope himself, the expediency of gratifying it is obvious on high political grounds. I trust that it may be within your power to gratify it. The gentlemen are believed to be in this City.

I have the honor to be, Sir,

Your obedient servant,

William H. Seward[9]

Why the secretary of state did not mention Joseph O'Keefe in the letter is somewhat puzzling, though perhaps simply an oversight. Or, it could be that the young man's personal credentials, as nephew of the Catholic Bishop of Ireland's County Cork, impressed Cardinal Antonelli, the Pope's secretary of state, enough to win O'Keefe a separate recommendation.

In securing the meeting with Seward, Keogh again showed the benefits of his upbringing, that confidence and assertiveness in moving among people of all levels. He and his colleagues had been promised commissions but the ranks were still to be decided. Ambitious as they were, each was hopeful that it be higher than lieutenant, the grade that all of them held in the Papal War. Their Papal medals would be a ready bargaining chip, if needed, at this opportune time when the Union army needed more officers.

. . .

As they wove their way through the upper echelons of government, it is thought that Keogh and his colleagues also met with President Lincoln.[10] He was well aware of the unification movement in Italy, particularly the accomplishments of the country's top military commander, Giuseppe Garibaldi, who he tried to recruit for the Union cause. Though that attempt had failed, later on a meeting with some of the men that his envoys recruited from the Papal War could easily have taken place with the President.

Lincoln had made a decided effort to recruit Garibaldi early in the Civil War. By the end of 1860, after the Italian militarist had succeeded in unifying the Kingdom of the Two Sicilies and, with that, most of Italy, he was essentially out of work. Coming to America to fight for the Union was not an impossible idea, but Lincoln's offer, command of one of the corps within the Union army, was not enough for Garibaldi.

He wanted the top position, command of all Union forces, and nothing less. He was also adamant that slavery be abolished immediately. Lincoln's intent, at that early stage in the Civil War, was to end the secession of southern states and preserve the Union. Freeing the slaves would come after that.[11] The two could not come to an agreement and Garibaldi stayed in Europe, focusing his considerable abilities on the further unification of his homeland.

Keogh, Kiely, and O'Keefe emerged from the meeting with Seward, each with the rank of captain in the Union's volunteer army. As a trained soldier with the ambition to make the military a career, Keogh likely wanted a commission in the regular U.S. Army. But with the onset of the war, the Union needed to rapidly increase its fighting force, and that was best achieved by inducting huge numbers into a volunteer army.

Initially, Lincoln called for 75,000 volunteers, more than four times the 16,000 men who made up the regular U.S. army in 1861. They were trained, competent soldiers but certainly not the numbers to fight the conflict that loomed. As well, the majority of the army were spread across the West beyond the Mississippi River.

The officers among them were mostly southerners, reflecting the South's tradition of military training and service, and once the southern states seceded, they switched their allegiance to the Confederacy,[12] in short order creating the Union's officer deficit. The President's call for volunteers brought men from all walks of life, but very few with any military experience. It made an experienced officer like Keogh, a member of the volunteer army himself, a valuable asset in working with the new recruits.

In late April 1862, Keogh and his friends left Washington for northern Virginia's Shenandoah Valley, joining Union troops pitted against Confederate forces in General Thomas J. "Stonewall" Jackson's Valley Campaign. They were assigned to the command of Brigadier General James Shields, Keogh as Shield's acting aide-de-camp.

The 52-year-old general had served in the Mexican War, and in a number of political posts including Governor of the Oregon Territory and, at different times, senator from Illinois, Minnesota, and Missouri. As a transplant from County Tyrone, Ireland, at about age 20,[13] the same age as Keogh when he set off for Italy, he and his young officer shared a personal background, certainly an element of comfort in Keogh's first battlefield assignment in the Civil War.

Jackson's troops had occupied the Shenandoah Valley, an important battle corridor for both sides, throughout the spring of 1862, moving north and south and engaging Union forces in a series of small battles. Though they outnumbered Rebel forces, the strategy kept some 60,000 Union troops spread out and unable to decisively beat the opposition and move against Richmond.[14]

As the Confederacy faced major defeats elsewhere—notably in

Tennessee at the forts of Henry and Donelson the previous winter, the vital port of New Orleans, and Seven Pines (also called Fair Oaks) in Virginia—for Jackson to have won six out of seven battles in the Valley campaign gave the South a much needed boost in morale.

The only Union victory, in late March, at Kernstown, Virginia, went to Shields, who bragged about his win against Jackson for the rest of his years.[15] Sidelined with an injury from that battle, he didn't return to his command until late April, about the time Keogh and his colleagues arrived in camp. Ahead for Shields was command of Union troops in what would be the final Valley engagement, the Battle of Port Republic on June 9, 1862. Hard-fought, each side suffered some 1,000 dead.[16]

In that battle, Captain Keogh's first in the Civil War, his bravery stood out. Military records noted that he and his horse, Tom, came under enemy fire from beginning to end of combat, both making it through without injury.[17] As far as is known, Tom was Keogh's first horse in the war and would be his partner until late in the conflict.

Commanding a mounted patrol prior to the Battle of Port Republic, Keogh very nearly captured General Jackson himself.[18] At the time, the general was headquartered with his staff in the town of Port Republic, on that Sunday morning, June 8, about to go to church. Jackson's horse, Little Sorrel, was already saddled up and the general made a hasty escape, though some members of his staff were captured.[19]

Thereafter, the Union raiders fell back until the next day, when Rebel forces succeeded in winning at Port Republic, and ending the Valley Campaign. With that victory, Jackson succeeded in pushing Union troops out of the Shenandoah Valley, thereby freeing up his troops to assist General Robert E. Lee in defense of the Confederacy's capitol. The achievements catapulted Jackson to fame among Civil War commanders.

Keogh was commended for his work, a promising start to his

American military career. Shields, however, did not fare as well. The day after the Union victory at Kernstown, Lincoln promoted him to major general. Other military officers disagreed with the President, raising questions about Shields' military abilities. Whatever the specific criticisms, Shields shouldered the ultimate Union defeat. His troops failed to hold ground against the Confederates at Port Republic and were forced to withdraw from the Shenandoah Valley. His promotion was rejected, and in 1863 Shields resigned his commission and left the U.S. Army.[20]

Sadly, the Shenandoah Campaign was the last time the three friends would fight together. Kiely was severely wounded, but he would recover and return to battle, to the Second Louisiana Cavalry.

Six weeks after the Battle of Port Republic, Keogh and O'Keefe also moved on, slated to serve as staff officers for Brigadier General John Buford, Jr. The general was regarded by many as the best cavalry officer in both the Union and Confederate armies[21], and serving with him was a valuable position for someone of Keogh's leadership and riding abilities. It would also be the beginning of an important personal relationship.

But the assignment was interrupted almost before it began. There was clearly an informal pipeline of sorts, a way for commanders to know the members of others' staffs, and who might be available for a transfer as needed. General George McClellan, commander of the Army of the Potomac, had been watching the two captains, Keogh and O'Keefe. Even though they had just begun their association with Buford, McClellan requested their transfer to his staff. Whatever their personal feelings, to be hired away by the head of the army was indicative of the reputation they were building.

KEOGH CAME TO THE CIVIL WAR IN ITS SECOND YEAR, AND FROM then he fought through to the end in more than 80 battles. Typical of the myriad engagements, most were small, but each was identified and recorded in detail, though many now are largely forgotten. But large and small, the battles he fought in read like a roadmap through the Civil War.

As the war settled into its second year, conflicts grew in number and intensity, the level of death and destruction at times almost beyond comprehension. It was variously called in the North, the War of Rebellion or the War of Southern Rebellion, and in the South, the War Between the States or the War of Northern Aggression, and remains today America's bloodiest conflict.

The war had started with the firing on the Federal garrison of Ft. Sumter, in Charleston harbor, South Carolina in the spring of 1861. It was looked upon as an insurrection, something that could be quelled before it got out of hand. The antecedents stretched back years as the slave-free northern states and the slave-owning southern states grappled with the right to have slaves in a country whose Declaration of Independence said "all Men are created equal."[22] Would slavery be allowed to continue in states where it already existed, but prohibited in the territories that would become future states? Or must it be abolished throughout the country?

Lincoln's 1860 campaign promise was that slavery would be prohibited in the territories, a pledge that pushed seven southern states to secede from the United States and form the Confederate States of America. South Carolina led the exodus on December 20, 1860, followed two months later by Mississippi, Florida, Alabama, Georgia, Louisiana, and Texas.Then on April 12, 1861, following Lincoln's inauguration, Confederate troops captured Fort Sumter, lowered the American flag and hoisted the Rebel "Stars and Bars."[23] With that the Civil War began.

In rapid succession, Lincoln's call for the first 75,000 volunteers for the army was followed by a Proclamation of Blockade of Confederate ports,[24] the latter to prevent the export of cotton to foreign countries and the smuggling of war supplies to the Rebels. Virginia seceded from the Union, followed by Arkansas, Tennessee, and North Carolina.

The Confederacy then numbered 11 states, with a population of some nine million people, four million of whom were slaves. The Union had 20 free states as war started, plus the allegiance of four Border States, states that allowed slavery but had not seceded from the Union. On June 20, 1863 West Virginia would become a state, joining as the fifth Border State. The Union population at the beginning of hostilities was estimated to be between 20 and 21 million people.

At the end of 1861, some one million men were under arms, ready to engage each other at points along a 1,200-mile battle corridor that stretched from Virginia to Missouri.[25] Victories that first year went to the Confederacy at First Bull Run (First Manassas) in Virginia and Wilson's Creek (Springfield) in Missouri. Dual names, when used, reflected the Union's choice to name battles for a waterway and the Confederate's preference for a town name. Victories and losses aside, fighting that first year was mild compared to the rest of the war.

FILLING THE RANKS ON BOTH SIDES WERE HUNDREDS OF THOUSANDS of immigrants, some 47 percent of the fighting force.[26] The largest groups were German and Irish, followed by Italians, French, Hungarians, Scandinavians, English, Canadians, Orientals, and more. Among them, some 170,000 Irish-born fought for both sides, about 150,000 for the Union and 20,000 for the Confederacy[27] both sides with equal passion and, in their way, fighting for the right of the colony against the mother power. Irish fighting for the Union felt they were preserving the country that broke with England 85 years before. Those in the South fought for their independence from the United States, not unlike Ireland's wish to be free of England or, as they might have said, the colony against the oppressive motherland.

The Irish had emigrated to the U.S. over many years, most recently during and after the Great Famine when the greatest numbers came looking for a new start in life. Arriving by the hundreds of thousands, the Irish were mostly unwelcome, as was (and is) the usual case for the newest group to arrive in an area, as they settled in, looked for work, and struggled to be accepted.

Immigrants joined the army, on one hand for reasons of patriotism, loyalty and gratitude to their new country, and on the other hand for the practicality of steady employment and a paycheck. Whatever the reason, as these men put their lives on the line for the cause, be it for north or south, their contributions eased the path to assimilation. Particularly in the North where the massive influx of Irish immigrants was most acutely felt, fighting in the Civil War lessened some of the negative feelings toward them.

Still, assimilation wasn't an easy road. Military units filled with native-born Americans were not welcoming, so with resolve they organized their own all-Irish militias. Loosely gathered under the Union Army's Irish Brigade, the mainstays were the 63rd, 69th, and 88th New York Infantry regiments, along with other predominantly Irish regiments from Massachusetts, Connecticut, Ohio, and Wisconsin.

However, with numbers as large as they were, it was not long before Irish-born recruits, of necessity, were being assigned to established Union companies other than the all-Irish ones.[28] Irish fighting for the Confederacy raised regiments in Tennessee and Alabama and, like their northern countrymen, joined many other non-Irish units. In all, more Irish joined the fight in the U.S. Civil War than at any point in history except World War I.[29]

Many Irishmen rose to become commanding officers, numerous among them achieving the rank of general, either through regular promotion or brevetting, a reward system that conferred a higher rank. Brevets could come with increased pay, authority, and uniform, but when they did not, the recipient was still called by the advanced rank.

Keogh served two Irish generals, Brigadier General James Shields in the Shenandoah Valley Campaign and before him, Major General John J. Coppinger, company commander in the Irish Battalion that fought through the Papal War.

A year ahead of Keogh, Coppinger also was recruited by Archbishop Hughes and Secretary of State Seward. He entered the Civil War as a captain in the 14th U.S. Infantry of the regular Union Army[29] and also served as cavalry commander of volunteers. Following the Civil War, he fought in the Indian wars in the Far West, mostly in California, and then in the Spanish-American War, in all serving 46 years in the U.S. military. In retirement, he penned a tribute to the three young men he had commanded in Italy so many years before:

> They came directly from Italy, where they were lieutenants in the Pope's service. They went directly to the field in Virginia. They fought, they died—these gallant Irish gentlemen—dear old boys—God bless them.[30]

The man that Keogh would work for in the summer of 1862, Major General George McClellan, or "Little Mac" as he was affectionately called by the men under his command, won the approval of President Lincoln early in the Civil War, the President at first commending McClellan's leadership in achieving Union victories, notably at Rich Mountain, West Virginia, and the First Battle of Bull Run in Virginia. In that same year, 1861, those successes also led to the President appointing him commander of the Army of the Potomac and then, upon the retirement of General Winfield Scott, general-in-chief of all Union forces.

As Lincoln said to McClellan, the supreme command "will entail a vast labor upon you. McClellan's reply, "I can do it all."[31] The exchange, in time, would point up the differences in how the two men viewed the conduct of war. The general's skill in organizing and caring for his men was widely acknowledged. He pressed for better military training for them, and was held in high esteem for the esprit de corps he engendered. His flaw was the cautiousness with which he sometimes led his men on the battlefield, delaying his attacks or allowing the enemy to retreat without further action. McClellan's mindset came to aggravate the President, eventually in the extreme.

In March 1862, as the Peninsula Campaign in Virginia got underway, Lincoln relieved McClellan as general-in-chief. Over the next four months, the President served as his own top commander, handling the direction of Union forces himself. Then in mid-July, he gave the job to Major General Henry Halleck. His abilities as a strategist on the battlefield were considered ineffective, but Lincoln was aware of Halleck's talents as a visionary and hoped he could orchestrate a more effective Union war effort.[32]

The savagery of the Civil War was unrelenting in its second year, Union and Confederate forces opposing each other repeatedly in small to large campaigns, some the huge battles whose names resonate still. Shiloh, on the Tennessee River, was a Rebel win in early April. Late the same month, the capture of New Orleans gave the Union control of the South's most important seaport. Then at the end of May, with another (albeit slim) Union victory in the Battle of Seven Pines near Richmond, the Confederacy made a major change. June 1, 1862, the day after Seven Pines ended the Peninsula Campaign, General Robert E. Lee took command of the Confederate army, renaming his Rebel forces the Army of Northern Virginia.

CAPTAIN KEOGH REPORTED TO GENERAL MCCLELLAN'S STAFF IN LATE July to find his boss sidelined. After the General's protracted siege of Rebel troops in Virginia's Peninsula Campaign, Lincoln relieved him not only as commander-in-chief of all Union forces, but also as

Commander of the Army of the Potomac. The last firing, as it turned out, was brief. In late August, at the Second Battle of Bull Run (Second Manassas), Major General John Pope's 75,000 troops were soundly defeated by General "Stonewall" Jackson's 55,000 Rebels and forced to retreat to Washington. With that, Pope was out and McClellan was back commanding the army, in time to face Lee's emboldened attempt to take the war north and invade the Union.

Lee's plan was to push into the Border State of Maryland. It would be the first time that Rebel troops would fight outside the Confederacy. Moving out of Virginia, Lee's forces headed 50 miles northwest of Washington, intent on disabling the Federal garrison at Harpers Ferry. Lincoln scrambled to pull together as many troops as he could from the Washington area, soldiers who had fought in the Peninsula Campaign and Second Bull Run, as well as fresh untrained and untested recruits. McClellan, drawing on his strengths, had Union forces organized and ready to pursue the Rebels in four days.[33] The imbalance was striking—90,000 Union troops ready to oppose 50,000 Rebels.

To stop the Confederate advance and gain a victory for the Union was suddenly very important. Lincoln believed he needed a win then to bolster his plan to issue the Emancipation Proclamation and free all slaves. He felt the Proclamation would add a moral purpose to the Union's desire to restore itself to its full size, and to keep the war on track in the face of burgeoning casualties.[34]

On September 4, 1862 Confederate troops crossed into Maryland. Their target was Harpers Ferry, just over the West Virginia line, a nexus of the Chesapeake & Ohio Canal and the Baltimore & Ohio railroad, both vital transportation resources for the Union. "Stonewall" Jackson captured Harpers Ferry, forcing the surrender of the garrison and capturing more than 12,500 troops.[35] Meanwhile, Union troops won the Battle of South Mountain west of Frederick, Maryland.

With the loss of South Mountain, Lee planned to return to

Virginia. But Jackson's win at Harpers Ferry gave him another choice, reason to stand and fight again on Union soil. He moved his troops west of Frederick to Sharpsburg, Maryland, setting the stage on September 17 for the Battle of Antietam (Sharpsburg), the bloodiest one-day battle in American history.

Savage combat extending over 12 hours involved both sides in numerous attacks and counterattacks, this despite the fact that Union forces were more than double Rebel forces. Of the more than 100,000 troops that fought, casualties were nearly 25 percent—men who were dead, injured, captured, or missing in action. At the end of the day, Union and Confederate troops were so battered and bloodied that on the following day both sides hunkered in place, neither side prepared to continue the fight.

The night of September 18, Lee withdrew his forces back to Virginia. There was one final clash at Shepherdstown, Virginia (now West Virginia), when pursuing Union troops were pushed back over the Potomac river by the Confederate rear guard. Other than that, General McClellan did not pursue Lee's forces. This was the final straw for Lincoln.

Historians generally call the Battle of Antietam a draw but, given Lee's retreat, the Union counted it as a victory. Four days later, on September 22, Lincoln issued the preliminary Emancipation Proclamation, stating that the Rebels must end their fighting and rejoin the Union by January 1, 1863—100 days hence—or all slaves in the Confederate states still in rebellion would be freed. When the deadline was not met, the Emancipation Proclamation went into effect, freeing 3.1 million of the nation's 4 million slaves.[36] Not freed at that time were slaves in the Border States of Maryland, Delaware, Kentucky, and Missouri, and in parts of the Confederacy under control of the Union army, namely Tennessee, lower Louisiana, and the counties in Virginia that would become West Virginia. The chance for a negotiated settlement was over. The war would be fought to a bitter end, slavery reinstated if the South won, slavery abolished if the

North won. For the Union, beyond the battle to bring the Confederate states back, now it was to provide freedom for all. Antietam expanded the reason for war.

As war continued, European governments that had considered alliances with the Confederacy now rejected the idea—and 200,000 African Americans joined the Union forces.[37] Their units, composed of men from various situations—Northern free blacks, runaway slaves and, later, freed slaves—were called United States Colored Troops, though they were also open to people other than African Americans.

But Antietam, Union win though it was, did not spare McClellan from Lincoln's ire. The President felt Little Mac should have taken the initiative to pursue Lee into Virginia. Dissatisfied with the battle outcome because of that, Lincoln visited the general in October at the Antietam battlefield, where the two sat in McClellan's tent, discussing their conflicting ideas. As the President put it to McClellan, "If you don't want to use the Army, I should like to borrow it for a while."[38]

Once Lincoln had made his travel plans, Keogh was chosen, along with five other soldiers, to be the President's military escort while he was at the battlefield. The visit did not go well for McClellan. Lincoln wanted a general who could defeat Lee and end the war[39] and Little Mac had shown himself unable to do that. On November 7, 1862, Lincoln relieved McClellan of his post, replacing him with Major General Ambrose Burnside as the new commander of the Army of the Potomac.

Gracious even in difficult times, the man his troops knew him to be, McClellan took the opportunity to write a generous compliment of Captain Keogh, as it would turn out, the first of many. He was, said the general,

> "....a most gentlemanlike man, of soldierly appearance ... whose

> record had been remarkable for the short time he had been in the army ... I was exceedingly glad to have him as an aide."[40]

General McClellan was ordered to Trenton, New Jersey to await further orders, but they never came. In 1864, he ran as the Democrat's candidate for President opposing his former Commander-in-Chief. He lost that election but 14 years later became Governor of New Jersey. In later years, McClellan wrote of his command of the Army of the Potomac, defending his decisions against Lincoln's, but died before the work could be published.

THEIR TIME WITH MCCLELLAN OVER, CAPTAINS KEOGH AND O'KEEFE soon rejoined General Buford's command, Keogh as one of the general's staff officers, a position that put him at the center of military operations. Leaders at every level of the military on both sides, from general of the army, to commanders of individual divisions, brigades, and regiments had such staffs to handle a range of responsibilities, from readying men for battle, to the logistics and supplies for travel and encampments. They were challenging positions that could change from the tedium of hand-copying a set of orders or other document to actually guiding a regiment into position in a battle already in progress.[41]

When he worked for General McClellan, Keogh was the acting aide-de-camp, a position considered a commander's confidential assistant, with duties that included writing and delivering of orders. Buford spoke of his ten staff officers, Keogh and three other captains, and six lieutenants,[42] but never indicated what particular responsibilities each handled or if these varied with each engagement. One thing is sure, Buford was encouraging, supportive, and quick to compliment the men in his command. Soon he and Keogh, 14 years his junior, developed a kinship, somewhat like that of a father and son, or an older and younger brother.

Born in Kentucky and raised in Rock Island, Illinois, Buford, like most of the generals in the Civil War, was a graduate of the U.S. Military Academy at West Point. Fresh from graduation, he requested assignment in the cavalry, which landed him with the U.S. Army's First and then Second Dragoons. In the Civil War, his talents, instincts, and bravery as a cavalryman were highly regarded and his assignments reflected that. He commanded a cavalry brigade under Major General John Pope in the Second Battle of Bull Run, then rose to chief of cavalry under General McClellan in the Maryland Campaign (Harpers Ferry, Frederick, and Antietam).[43]

Keogh's battlefield association with Buford began with the Battle of Fredericksburg in Virginia, fought December 13, 1862. Buford continued as chief of cavalry in General Burnside's first battle commanding the Army of the Potomac, a battle that would go down in history as the largest concentration of forces in the Civil War. Yet, despite overwhelming Union strength—120,000 of its troops to 80,000 Confederate troops—it was a costly Union defeat to the tune of almost 13,000 casualties. The numbers, well over double Confederate losses,[44] greatly raised southern spirits after Lee's defeat at Antietam. Fredericksburg was also the end of Burnside's brief command of the Army of the Potomac. In January 1863, Lincoln replaced him with Major General Joseph Hooker.

Forces faced off again in Virginia at Chancellorsville, where General Lee's divide and conquer tactics won what many consider his greatest victory against the larger Union force. Through the late winter, Hooker reorganized and refitted the Army of the Potomac, improving food, medical care, and leave for the soldiers.[45] He also expanded Buford's role, promoting him to commander of the Cavalry Corps, Reserve Brigade, First Division.

But Lee's persistence in attacking vulnerable portions of Hooker's forces in early May 1863, gave the South this second important win.

The battle was also marked by the devastating loss of Lee's star commander, General "Stonewall" Jackson, mistakenly shot by friendly fire. Despite Hooker's efforts to improve the army, after his loss at Chancellorsville he resigned his command, though he continued to serve in other theaters of operation during the Civil War. At the end of June, Lincoln named Major General George Meade to command the Army of the Potomac, the fifth man to do so in less than a year.[46]

PRE-WAR AND, INDEED, THROUGH THE EARLY PART OF THE CIVIL WAR, the cavalry was looked upon as an elitist part of the army, used in mostly peripheral ways such as for patrols, scouting, protecting pack trains and railroads, and to escort generals from point to point. Its rarified image prompted the foot soldiers' sneer that one never saw a dead cavalryman.[47] By mid-war, however, that remark rang hollow as dead cavalrymen and their horses piled up on battlefields along with dead infantrymen. The cavalry's role had evolved to be a viable fighting force, never more so than on June 9, 1863 at the Battle of Brandy Station in Virginia, where the largest predominantly cavalry battle ever fought in North America occurred.

Buford, a student of cavalry theory and tactics while at West Point, pressed for the increased involvement of the cavalry, convinced that it would be more valuable as a mounted infantry.[48] Combined with General Hooker's work in the months prior to Brandy Station, to upgrade the cavalry by bringing together various units under a single corps, at Brandy Station the Union finally had enough cavalry power to compete on par with their southern counterparts.[49]

Lee had been moving his battered troops through northern Virginia, looking for food and supplies, all the while pushing north to take the fight to Union soil. Major General J.E.B Stuart, his cavalry commander, was screening Lee's forces from detection until in the area of Brandy Station, Stuart's presence was discovered by General

Buford, who was leading one wing of the First Division Cavalry. Of more than 21,000 combatants who squared off, the overwhelming number were mounted troops.

After 14 hours of combat, Major General Alfred Pleasanton, commander of the Cavalry Corps, directed Buford to withdraw his troops, ending the battle in a narrow defeat for the Union. Buford lost some ten percent of his force,[50] but in terms of encouragement for the cavalry, it was anything but a defeat. Or as Stuart's chief aide said, "Brandy Station made the Federal Cavalry."[51]

Brandy Station was the opening battle of the Gettysburg Campaign. It was also the end for that trio of young Irishmen—Keogh, Kiely, and O'Keefe—who sailed from their homeland to fight in the American Civil War. O'Keefe was wounded and captured, from there sent to a Confederate prison. Kiely, recuperated, was with the Second Louisiana Cavalry. Keogh, now on his own, continued on Buford's staff.

As forces pushed farther north, they clashed again at Upperville, Virginia two weeks later. The outcome was inconclusive but Buford, proud of his men's performance, said, "I'll be damned if I can't whip a little corner of Hell with that First Brigade."[52]

JUST OVER THE PENNSYLVANIA LINE WAS THE TOWN OF GETTYSBURG, site of a battle that would earn superlatives as both the largest battle of the Civil War and the largest ever fought in North America. It lasted from July 1 to July 3, 1863, and involved 165,000 men, 85,000 from the Union and 75,000 from the Confederacy. Casualties were horrendous, more than one-quarter of northern forces and more than one-third of southern forces. The Union win would not turn the tide immediately, but the Battle of Gettysburg was a decisive victory, that sealed the fate of the Confederacy.

Under General Meade, commanding the Army of the Potomac, Buford was now in charge of the whole First Division Cavalry. In that first day, as troops from both sides moved toward their destination, Buford had the foresight and experience to impede the advance of some of Lee's troops, holding a high ground in the vicinity of what are now known as Cemetery Ridge and Little Round Top until Union troops arrived.[53] The maneuver occurred on a road running west from Gettysburg to Cashtown. As Buford moved his horsemen into the area the day before, he and some of his officers scouted roads and interviewed local residents, the information they gathered convincing Buford that fighting would start the next day, July 1.

Early that morning, Buford positioned dismounted cavalrymen along the road, where they put up a resistance and slowed the progress of Major General Henry Heth's Rebel forces. It was a persistent, paced blocking measure that bought time for Major General John Reynolds to move the infantry in, taking the coveted high ground east and south of the town by sundown. Buford's forces were ordered to move south of Gettysburg on the second day to tend to the horses and regroup. One of his brigades fought on the third day, incurring heavy losses.[54]

Buford and his men pursued Lee's retreating forces for ten days, the cavalry moving ahead of the infantry, harassing the Rebels, clashing at Boonsboro, Funkstown, Hagerstown, and elsewhere.[55] It was the follow-through that Lincoln wanted at Antietam and, doubtless, approved of now. But masses of dead cavalrymen and their horses laying on final battlefields were hard for even the toughest soldiers to look at. The old infantry dig about never seeing a dead cavalryman no longer made sense.

What Buford masterminded, in delaying the enemy long enough for Union forces to move in and stop their advance, contributed to the outcome at Gettysburg. But a modest man who dodged praise and accolades, Buford was always more interested in commending his staff for their performance, as he did in his report on the cavalry's actions at Gettysburg:

> My staff—Captains Norris, Keogh, Wadsworth, and Bacon, and Lieutenants Mix, P. Penn Gaskill, Dean, Morrow, Wing, and Gilchrist—were always on hand, and gave me much valuable information from where the fire was hottest, and were of immense assistance in conveying orders on the field of battle, and seeing that they were obeyed. During the campaign they were all under heavy fire on different occasions, and for coolness and gallantry cannot be excelled in this army.[56]

Buford was equally complimentary to all the men in his command, and offered his brigade commanders "my heartfelt thanks for their zeal and hearty support." Captain Keogh received his first brevet, to the rank of major, for his performance during the battle, the wording likely praising his efficiency and bravery.[57] Buford also gave him a commendation.[58]

The following day, July 4, Vicksburg on the Mississippi River fell to the Union. General Ulysses S. Grant, commanding the Army of the West, accepted the surrender of General John Pemberton after a six-week siege. The Mississippi River was now in Union hands and the Confederacy was effectively split, further sealing its doom.

THE FORCES THAT MET AT GETTYSBURG REPAIRED THEMSELVES through the summer and early fall. Then through October and early November 1863, they again pursued each other through central and northern Virginia, in a series of skirmishes and battles known as the Bristoe Campaign. General Lee, attempting to reach Washington, found his progress blocked by General Meade as he moved back to the Capitol, supported by Buford's cavalry. The two battles, at Bristoe Station and Rappahannock Station were both Union victories. The campaign was General Buford's last.

That fall, at his headquarters in Culpepper, Virginia, colleagues saw Buford struggling against fatigue bordering on exhaustion, and the arthritis in his back from many years in the saddle also growing more painful. Dismissive about what ailed him as just part of a soldier's life, he fought against his worsening condition. But on November 21 the 37-year-old general relinquished his command and went on sick leave.[59] The diagnosis, when it came, was severe typhoid fever.

In early December 1863, Captain Keogh accompanied his commander to Washington, where Buford's old friend, General George Stoneman, put his home at their disposal. Over the next several days, Buford's illness worsened rapidly, his fatigue from earlier in the fall sapping any strength to fight. Keogh stayed at his friend's bedside throughout his ordeal as other colleagues gathered around them.

Near the end, Stoneman pushed for Buford to be promoted to the rank of major general, and on December 16, President Lincoln agreed. He wrote:

> I am informed that General Buford will not survive the day. It suggests itself to me that he will be made Major General for distinguished and meritorious service at the Battle of Gettysburg.[60]

Keogh presented Buford with his promotion, backdated to July 1, 1863, helped him sign the paperwork, then co-signed it.[61] Buford was passing in and out of delirium and Keogh had to convince him that his promotion was genuine. But in a lucid moment, as he understood the truth, he said only, "It is too late. Now I wish I could live."[62]

Keogh was holding Buford in his arms as he died at two o'clock, the afternoon of December 16. Ever the soldier, as he passed he must have drifted back to the battlefield to again command his troops, his last words being, "Put guards on all the roads and don't let the men run to rear."[63] With his death, Keogh had lost a father, older brother, mentor, and cherished friend. He was devastated.

President Lincoln attended Buford's memorial service in Washington four days later. Grey Eagle, Buford's white horse from Gettysburg was part of the military escort.[64] After, Captain Keogh took his general's body by train to the U.S. Military Academy at West Point where he was interred. In the next plot is a fellow Gettysburg hero, Lieutenant Alonzo Cushing, killed in action at age 22 while holding the high ground that Buford first secured.[65] The general would have liked that.

Chapter 4

CARRYING ON

KEOGH RETURNED TO WASHINGTON TO ACCEPT AN OFFER THAT WOULD brighten his winter and set him on a new and different course. General Stoneman, who had kept vigil with Keogh at Buford's bedside, asked the captain to join him in his new role as cavalry commander of the Western Theater. With the beginning of 1864, Keogh would be his aide-de-camp, the beginning of an association that would endure through the rest of the Civil War and beyond.

Perhaps it was because Keogh's family was far away, his parents dead, his brothers and sisters back in Ireland. But whatever it was, he had found, and now lost, a true and honest friend in Buford, and he was taking all of it very hard. Still, Stoneman and he had developed a rapport through those difficult days in December. The two had likely met through Buford during the war, as Buford and Stoneman had been friends since their days at West Point. Now the connection was growing, and Keogh went with the positive feeling he had.

From his perspective, Stoneman saw a compassionate man, committed and caring enough to stay at his friend Buford's side throughout his ordeal. He was taken with Keogh's generosity and honesty, a willingness to extend himself and to show his feelings. As

Buford had known, Stoneman was sure this was a man he wanted on his team.

Stoneman was 18 years older than Keogh. An easterner raised in New York State, he migrated west as an adult and fell in love with California. His army career began on the frontier, where he fought in Indian wars in California and Oregon, then with the 5th U.S. Cavalry in the Mexican War. Stoneman was in command of Fort Brown, Texas, at the outbreak of the Civil War, but within months had joined McClellan's staff to fight in the east. In July 1861, when the general became commander of the Army of the Potomac, Stoneman became Chief of Cavalry.[1]

For the second time, Keogh was casting his lot with the cavalry. Stoneman, like Buford, was committed to the concept of mounted soldiers and the strengths they brought to the battlefield, a belief begun for both at West Point. Stoneman was two years ahead of Buford, graduating in 1846 with the class whose members, besides his future boss, McClellan, included later Civil War leaders, Samuel Sturgis, George Pickett, and Stoneman's roommate, "Stonewall" Jackson.[2]

Two years later, when Hooker was in command of the Army, he put Stoneman in charge of the entire Cavalry Corps. (Buford commanded one of the corps' three divisions.) But in June 1863, following the Confederate victory at Chancellorsville, Hooker spread the blame for the loss and he sent Stoneman to Washington to head the newly-formed Cavalry Bureau. Stoneman's achievement in building and operating the mammoth Giesboro Point, D.C. horse depot, a pipeline for procuring, housing, and training upward of 20,000 horses at a time (and the largest of six depots that supplied Union forces), was a boon in a period when the supply of mounts was diminishing. Adjacent to the horse facilities, housing for troops waiting for remounts was nicknamed Camp Stoneman.[3] But within a few months, despite his success, Stoneman had his fill of bureaucracy and administrative work. After Buford died, he prevailed upon his friend, Major General John Schofield, to help him get back to the battlefield and the action he longed for.

Once he had returned from Buford's internment at West Point, Keogh made a short trip to Culpepper, Virginia, 70 miles south of the Capitol. Buford's staff and troops were still encamped there, and he wanted to check on the horses. Months ago, he had been looking forward to a convivial time between their commander, the staff and troops, as winter lay-ups usually were. It should have been a time for rank and file to enjoy a measure of camaraderie, taking stock, and looking to their participation in spring campaigns. Now there would be none of that. It wasn't just Keogh who missed Buford. All his men did. But the sense of sadness, in a curious way, may have made it easier for Keogh to leave and head back to Washington. Tom and the other horses were being well cared for, and he would be back for his trusted partner very soon.

Snow, ice, and frigid temperatures, so often the norms for winter, brought fighting to a standstill, or nearly so. True, over the course of the war, a handful of major battles were fought between November and March—Chattanooga, Fredericksburg, Nashville, Stones River, Roanoke Island, Forts Henry and Donelson, and Pea Ridge—but most units bedded down and waited for the season to melt into spring.

Winter camps were pitched most anywhere, on people's farms and open lands, to provide shelter for officers, troops, and horses. Some were attractively organized with cabins in symmetrical rows, others a ramshackle array of tents, cabins, and log-and-canvas hybrids.[4] It was rough living, a long, cold, dug-in variation on the rigors of the campaign seasons. Still, soldiers did the best they could to make the life as tolerable as possible. Cabins were simple affairs built of hewn logs, the interior furnishings of whatever was available. Floors were mostly dirt, some sunken for added warmth. If bricks were available, there might even be a chimney. The men kept warm any way they could, some sleeping fully dressed, others sharing a bunk with another for the extra body heat and the second blanket that provided.[5]

Not surprisingly, winter camp for the officers was more comfortable than for the men under them. Keogh, who entered the Civil War as a captain, would have had his own cabin or, if he chose, shared the space with one other officer, as opposed to three or more. The exterior was also of logs, but the floors were wooden and the furnishings more refined, the bed, table and chairs even purchased locally. Everyone in camp enjoyed better food during such periods, served up by a cook working in his own mess tent, turning out fare that was considerably improved from the individual rations eaten by soldiers on the move.

For Keogh and his fellow officers, weather permitting, training and drilling their troops was the order of the day. Men were sent to fighting units with minimal combat training, and winter camp was an extended period for them to learn what would be required of them when the weather warmed and they squared off on the battlefield. Hours at a time, soldiers practiced the various formations of close-order drill, learning discipline and teamwork. Marching, falling in and out of line, handling weapons while standing shoulder to shoulder, and wheeling as a unit in response to attacks from other sides were all maneuvers that built effectiveness as a fighting force. Winter was also the time for target practice, one-on-one combat training, and engaging in full-scale mock battles. When they moved out in the spring, the men often burned their camp, the intent being that the enemy should find nothing that it could occupy at a later date.[6]

KEOGH STAYED IN THE CAPITOL THROUGH THE WINTER OF 1864, A continuing guest at Stoneman's house, as he began work with other officers on the general's staff. In late January 1864, the general briefly took command of an infantry corps in Knoxville, Tennessee. Then two months later he was tapped for the far more impressive position, commander of the entire Cavalry Corps attached to the Department of the Ohio, the latter under the direction of Schofield. Keogh, at the same time, received his brevet promotion to major in the volunteer army.[7]

Following Stoneman would put Keogh in a new part of the country, the section known as the Western Theater, one of the three main regions within which the Civil War was fought. It stretched from west of the Appalachian Mountains to the Mississippi River, and contained the vital corridor through which Union forces pushed into the agriculture-rich heart of the South, in the end one of the final blows to the Confederacy.

East of the Appalachians was the Eastern Theater, where Keogh had fought exclusively up to that point. It covered Virginia and Pennsylvania, the opposing capitols of Washington and Richmond, and was the most densely populated and highly industrial area. The third zone, called the Trans-Mississippi Theater, covered Missouri, Arkansas, Louisiana, Texas, present-day Oklahoma, Colorado and New Mexico.

TWENTY MONTHS AFTER KEOGH FIRST SAW WASHINGTON, IT WAS NOW a very different city, transformed by its central role in the war effort. Capturing the Union capitol was a continuing goal of the Confederates, and Lincoln was equally adamant that its defense be paramount. A force of between 15,000 and 50,000 troops were always on alert in the area (often at the annoyance of commanders who needed reinforcements in the field),[8] and with the city's 37-mile fortified perimeter nearing completion, Washington would be one of the world's best protected cities. Before the war was over, the ring of defense--the 68 forts, 20 miles of trench lines, gun and rifle pits, and 800 cannons circling the city--would stand the test.[9] In June 1864, General Jubal Early and his Rebel force advanced to within five miles of the White House and were repulsed.

Washington was also the prime medical destination for the casualties of battles in the Eastern Theater, hundreds of thousands of whom flooded the city's hospitals. In one day, during the worst of the fighting in the June 1864 Battle of Cold Harbor in Virginia, hospitals took in 17,717 patients.[10] From a single general hospital when war began, by that point there were over 100 military hospitals staffed by huge numbers of surgeons and nurses, many of the latter women who left their homes and volunteered to care for sick and injured soldiers, as well as the increasing needs of the Capitol's resident population. Women had long been the caregivers, but until well into the 19th century sick care was mostly family oriented and undertaken at home. The demands of the Civil War changed that and women stepped up to help. It set in motion the continued call for hospital care, and with that the need for trained nurses and the establishment of nursing schools.

But this small, antebellum city that was the root of many changes, at the same time saw its infrastructure crack under the weight of excessive demand, the drinking water polluted by sewage causing epidemics of smallpox, typhoid fever, and other diseases. The thousands of deaths touched the highest levels when Lincoln's son, Willie, succumbed to typhoid fever, and the President suffered nearly the same fate from smallpox.

Beyond the hospital boom, the war effort had a voracious need for physical space around the Washington area. As the main supplier of arms and ammunition, horses, food, and other provisions for the Army of the Potomac, Washington built huge warehouses, along with the mammoth horse depot, all of them fronting along the Potomac River. Across the city, more than 400 structures went up for the military and growing Federal government, including buildings for the departments of War and the Navy, and headquarters for the Union Army, the Army of the Potomac, and the Defenses of Washington.[11]

AS THE CIVIL WAR MOVED INTO THE FINAL FIFTEEN MONTHS, THE Union employed a strategy designed to bring about the total capitulation by the Confederacy. The goal was to destroy the South and its ingrained institution of slavery, and to restore the Union, giving it, as Lincoln said in his *Gettysburg Address*, "a new birth of freedom." Yet, Confederate forces continued to fight ferociously, even as they faced diminishing manpower and horsepower, and the odds of overall victory turned against them. Through the late spring and summer of 1864, brutal battles were waged in Virginia at The Wilderness, Spotsylvania, and Cold Harbor. Only the last was a Rebel victory. To the Union's advantage, Lincoln promoted General Ulysses Grant from head of Western armies to commander of all Union forces, a change that increased the North's relentless pressure to end the war.

Ahead for Stoneman and his troops was the enormous push through the south, in its magnitude one of the keys to bringing the South to its knees. It would begin with the Atlanta Campaign, the grand design of General William Tecumseh Sherman, who replaced Grant as commander of western forces in March 1864. The plan was for Sherman's forces to capture Atlanta and, from there, move across the Carolinas to the port of Savannah on the Atlantic Ocean. Reviled by the South, praised by the North, the devastating swath cut by troops went down in history as "Sherman's March to the Sea."

As preparations got underway, Stoneman readied the cavalry. New brigades were needed, which meant herds of fresh horses to supply them. He and Keogh headed for prime horse country, the farms around Lexington, Kentucky, to organize and train riders and horses into three cavalry units. At the end of April, the two rode out in front of 2,000 mounted troops with orders from Sherman to deliver cavalry to Knoxville and Chattanooga, Tennessee by the first week in May.[12]

Away from the East Coast, Keogh was rubbing shoulders with a new type of soldier, initially with a less than favorable reaction on their part. At Stoneman's headquarters, the escort service was made up of men from Company D, Seventh Ohio Cavalry, commanded by Captain Theodore Allen. Ohio soldiers saw themselves as harder riding and altogether tougher than their polished eastern counterparts, a comparison they relished. This particular group had all been recruited from the river towns along the Ohio River, and had named their unit the River Regiment. The new captain in their midst, as they saw it, was too smooth, too refined and, simply put, didn't fit in.

From their standpoint, it was easy to understand. At just over six feet, Keogh stood a half-head taller than the average soldier who, at the time, was about five foot eight inches. He was handsome, slender, and long-legged, and an elegant, accomplished rider. His uniforms were well-tailored and fitted him perfectly, and he moved with an air of confidence, what one might describe as being comfortable in one's skin.

Years later, as Allen remembered those early days with Keogh, he acknowledged that his men didn't extend much of a welcome. "There was altogether too much style," he said, recalling Keogh's centaur-like bearing on a horse, his spotless uniform that "fitted him like the skin of a sausage.We gave him the 'cold shoulder' and as he passed us snide remarks were passed, such as 'I wonder if his mother cuts his hair?'" Perhaps most harshly, one of the most basic gestures of camaraderie was withheld as no one offered him a drink from their canteen.[13]

The other side of the story, if there was one, has never been told. It was a busy time for Stoneman and Keogh, now the general's acting chief of staff, and perhaps Keogh didn't put much early effort into building a relationship with the men of the cavalry. Or perhaps he was the first native-born Irishman with a heavy brogue that the troops had met and, initially, he understood that they felt uncomfortable. Keogh, it would seem, generally kept his own counsel and, in this instance, merely bided his time.

As the Atlanta Campaign unfolded, Stoneman's cavalry brigades, totaling almost 4,000 riders, and Sherman's massive infantry force of 100,000 troops crossed the Tennessee River and began moving southward into Georgia. They battled Rebel fighters as they marched, finally engaging them at Resaca, not quite half way to Atlanta. It was mid-May 1864, and this was the first serious confrontation of the campaign. They were stopped in north Georgia hill country, and Stoneman ordered Keogh to organize an assault on a wooded knoll where Confederate troops were dug in.[14] As it turned out, it was Keogh's time to change the perception.

Stoneman put four companies of a battalion at Keogh's disposal, a total of 300 men. Ordering the riders to line up in columns, one for each company, Keogh moved to the front and picked up a fast trot. Disregarding incoming fire, he stood up in the stirrups, waved his cap over his head and, turning back to his men, yelled, "Hip, hip, hurrah, boys. Here we go!" With that he urged Tom, his trusted mount, into a gallop, the battalion surging forward behind them. The enemy, resistant to previous attempts to dislodge them from the hillside, buckled as Keogh and his men charged into their midst, taking most of them prisoner.

Thereafter, the tone in camp did an about face. Keogh's stylish, some even said dapper image, was no longer an issue. From then on, he was welcomed at every campfire, and offered drinks from canteens throughout the regiment.[15] The battle of Resaca was considered a Confederate victory because Union forces were unable to break through enemy lines. Keogh and his riders didn't change the official outcome, but their successful assault on a Rebel position, would certainly have brought credit to Union efforts and to Keogh personally.

Northern forces pressed on into the summer, heading south by southeast as they destroyed railroad lines and industrial works in their path, all the while tightening the noose around Atlanta. As Stoneman's riders swung west, they met Rebel forces at Dallas, the ensuing battle there giving Keogh his second brevet for leadership and bravery, a promotion to lieutenant colonel in the volunteer army.

Now close to Atlanta, Stoneman proposed a raid that would take his men south behind enemy lines to free Union prisoners at two Confederate prisons, Camp Oglethorpe at Macon, and Camp Sumter, better known as the dreaded Andersonville, in the town of the same name. The prisons spelled a death knell for thousands of soldiers held within their walls, and though the risks of a raid were high, Sherman told Stoneman that if the men achieved their goal, people everywhere would be grateful.[16]

The plan began well enough, Stoneman and better than 2,000 cavalrymen plus an artillery unit laying waste to more targets as they closed in on Macon. But as they approached the edge of town, dug in Confederate troops blocked their further advance. After a night of skirmishes, Stoneman's renewed attempts to break through enemy lines faltered. With troop morale also falling and Rebels closing around them, he ordered those who wished to save themselves to try to do so, an action that spared many troops.[17]

Keogh remained with his commander, as did some 500 cavalry, returning Confederate fire and covering the retreat of the majority of the Union forces. Near the end, a Rebel shell came within inches of wounding Stoneman but, instead, hit his horse, Beauregard. A pre-Civil War gift to the general, Beauregard had served him from the beginning of combat and now, with a gut shot, he was dead. Mounting another horse, Stoneman retreated to a church yard and sent a flag of surrender to the enemy.[18]

For Keogh, one more, very personal event marred the day. Tom was also killed, struck down from under his rider by Rebel fire. The sadness came less than a month after the horse, with the instincts of a long-time partner, saved Keogh's life. Though there was little time to mourn the loss in the midst of war, he would write touchingly of Tom, in a letter to his sister, Ellen, back in Ireland:

> "... my old charger that had carried me through so many dangers since the Battle of Port Republic, when Keily was wounded. I wish you could have seen the poor fellow, how he could leap, and on the 4th July he saved my life. Whilst riding on a bye road carrying an order I suddenly rode into a heavy outlying picket of the enemy.

> Tom saw them as they rose up to deliver their fire and jumped sideways over a wood fence into the wood skirting the road. He carried me safely out of range. I shall never have a horse like him again."[19]

It would be a few years before it happened. But another great horse would indeed partner with Keogh.

THEY WERE THE ENGINES OF THE CIVIL WAR, THE MILLIONS OF horses that were procured for the fight, to carry the infantry to battle and the cavalry through it, to haul artillery, and wagons loaded with all the other equipment of war. Statistics vary widely, but it is safe to say that the number of horses in the North and the South combined was several million. Over the next four years, their fate would be abysmal, their numbers decimated as more than a million horses and mules died, huge numbers in battle, even more from poor care and disease before they ever got to the battlefield.

The fortunate ones, like Tom and Beauregard, and many more, were cherished, loved, and cared for in every way possible. In death, when it so often came, they were mourned and remembered for what they had done. The less fortunate were looked upon as totally expendable, simply a conveyance on four limbs. Their riders did what was necessary for them, but with dispatch and often under the watchful eyes of others. When these horses died their riders got another, either from regimental stock or, if need be, appropriated from a local owner. If none could be had, the soldier walked to his next battle, sullen and complaining about his bad luck.

It didn't take long for the President to get involved to improve the horses' situation. From the beginning of the war, Lincoln was appalled at what the horses endured, and in May 1861, authorized the War Department to appoint a veterinarian for each of the six cavalry regiments in existence, the individual given a monthly salary of $17.00 and the rank of sergeant.[20] Within two years, the position would be elevated to require a veterinary surgeon, who would carry the rank of sergeant major and be paid the very handsome salary of $75.00 a month. Neither position would make much difference at the time, given the burgeoning numbers of horses that quickly became involved in the Civil War. But they were steps in the evolution of equine care, and would begin to improve the lot of the horses who came after the war.

Before Lincoln stepped in, there was not one veterinarian attached to any unit in the Army. Farriers, to the contrary, had been officially with the Army since 1792, when Congress legislated that the four existing cavalry units should each have one farrier.[21] While their job was to nail on shoes, many did what they could to treat the horses medically, something they continued in the Civil War. But overall, rudimentary medical care, and resting and rehabilitating horses in reserve camps was the extent of what could be done for them when they faltered. The humane treatment for injuries and disease was usually a clean, mortal gunshot.

STONEMAN AND KEOGH, AND THE OFFICERS WHO STOOD WITH THEM IN their attempted raid made it to Camp Oglethorpe in Macon, but not as liberators. They entered the prison as inmates on August 1, 1864. Oglethorpe was an officers' prison that held, at the time, its maximum population of 2,300 prisoners. Conditions were very poor, inadequate shelter, meager rations, and lack of sanitation fostering chronic dysentery and scurvy.[22]

Stoneman and Keogh were only there ten days, shipped out of the area with most of the other prisoners because of encroaching Union raids. The two spent the rest of their incarceration in South Carolina at the Old Charleston City Jail along with hundreds more soldiers, some housed inside but many more in the outside courtyard under worn and leaky tents.[23]

At the end of September, Stoneman and Keogh had the good luck to be released as part of a prisoner swap, their freedom specifically requested by Sherman. The gesture may have been encouraged by Keogh's friend, O'Keefe, who suggested his uncle, the Bishop of Cork, ask the Bishop of Charleston if he would put in a good word. Stoneman and Keogh had survived the brutal treatment, in part through their own cunning. Both had concealed money in their clothing that they used to purchase additional food, "about 8 dollars each day to keep from starving," Keogh said in another letter to Ellen, adding how grateful he was that Sherman had thought well enough of him to ask for his release, because he doubted he could have lasted much longer.[24]

None of the Civil War prisons, Union or Confederate, survived the conflict with anything approaching a reputation for humane treatment, the conditions in every one of them subpar by degrees from dismal to horrendous. All levels of care disintegrated as the war went on and the numbers of prisoners increased, particularly in the South where the breakdown of the war machine was sapping money that would have gone to run the prisons, however badly. The results, of course, magnified the horrors of malnutrition, starvation, disease, and the manner of death.

Unfortunately, the rank and file who stood with the officers in the failed Macon raid, went to Andersonville, considered one of, if not the worst of the Confederate prisons. By August 1864, 33,000 prisoners were held in a massive outdoor pen, some 260 acres in size, surrounded by a high stockade fence from the top of which sentries fired on prisoners who stepped out of line. In the 14 months it existed, 45,000 Union soldiers were imprisoned at Andersonville, and almost 13,000 (29%) died there.[25] One person was executed for war crimes conducted during the Civil War, the commandant of Andersonville,

Captain Henry Wirz. He was tried and found guilty by a military tribunal, and hanged on November 10, 1865 in Washington, D.C.[26]

KEOGH WAS NOT THERE FOR THE SURRENDER OF ATLANTA ON SEPT. 2, 1864, and the fire that engulfed the city, nor the dug-in fighting that continued for the next two months as the Confederates attempted to push Sherman's army out of the area. Nor was he a part of Sherman's infamous March to the Sea, that left behind a swath of destruction 300 miles long and 60 miles wide, ending with the capture of Savannah, Georgia, just before Christmas. Temporarily, one might say, he was unfit for combat, in need of time to recuperate after the weeks in prison. Thankfully, though, he left the Old Charleston City Jail under his own power, something we can deduce because within a week he and Stoneman were guests at a celebratory dinner at General Sherman's headquarters.[27]

It took a couple of months to regain his health, likely back in Washington, but by the late fall of 1864, Keogh had resumed his position, now Stoneman's permanent chief of staff. As had been the case at other points in his career, his performance alongside Stoneman had been watched by another commander. This time it was General Philip Sheridan, Chief of Cavalry for the Army of the Potomac, who wanted Keogh on his staff, specifically to command the Third New Jersey Cavalry, a unit within George Custer's division.[28] He and Custer had met earlier, when both served on McClellan's staff and, apparently, Custer was also anxious to have Keogh's services. There was no question that to return to the Eastern Theater and its army would be a prestigious move, and even Stoneman generously encouraged him though the loss would be at the general's expense.[29]

It was evident that Sheridan was not easily dissuaded, given that he allowed others to do what they could to persuade Keogh. One was his friend, Joseph O'Keefe, already on Sheridan's staff, who wrote to Keogh's brother, Tom, relaying to him how interested the general was,[30] apparently with the hope that Tom might convince his brother to join Sheridan's staff.

But flattering as the offer was, not to mention the extent that others went in trying to persuade him, Keogh chose to stay with Stoneman. He felt he was a good man, someone he respected and, as he had with Buford, he looked to the individual more than the promotion. He would continue on as he was.

THE WAR MOVED INTO ITS LAST FEW MONTHS, THE NORTH FIGHTING fiercely to end the conflict as the South, with dwindling troops and supplies, struggled just as hard to hang on. Stoneman was given the go-ahead to lead a raid from Tennessee into southwest Virginia. Keogh headed back to Lexington where he pulled together troops and horses for two brigades and sent them to Knoxville. From there, as Sherman was closing in on Savannah to the southeast, Stoneman pushed north with almost 6,000 cavalrymen,[31] destroying industrial works and infrastructure, and scattering every Confederate force that tried to stop them.

They were redeeming actions, as smoothly executed as the previous summer's were disastrous, and they proceeded quickly. Before the year was out, Keogh was back in Knoxville. Even though the fighting was almost over, winter had called a time out. Only two Confederate forces were left in the fight, Lee's army under siege at Petersburg, Virginia, and General Joseph Johnston's forces in Tennessee. Opposing them, Union forces numbered some 280,000 men.[32]

In swift final steps, Grant's troops broke through the Rebel lines at Petersburg on April 2, ending the 10-month siege. The same day the Confederate government, remaining soldiers, and what citizens had the means evacuated Richmond, heading south on the last functioning railroad from there, the Richmond and Danville line. Those who remained watched in horror as fires set by the retreating Rebel troops destroyed the center city. Union troops entered Richmond the next morning and raised the Stars and Stripes, after which Grant informed Lincoln that the Confederate capitol had been taken.

Seven days later, on April 9, 1865, Lee surrendered the Confederate army to Grant in the parlor of a farmhouse in the village of Appomattox Court House, Virginia. Grant's generous terms of surrender pardoned all officers and men, and allowed them to keep their personal property, most importantly their horses and mules which would be needed for a late spring planting. In addition, officers were allowed to keep their sidearms. Grant also sent three days rations to all of Lee's men. The war was officially over.

Scattered battles continued for weeks after Lee's surrender, erupting in pockets across the south and west. The last occurred on May 12 and 13 in Texas, the Battle of Palmito Ranch near Brownsville.[33] Keogh himself fought his final battle three days after the surrender, at Salisbury, North Carolina. He had ridden from Tennessee into North Carolina with Stoneman and the 6,000 cavalrymen in late March, prepared to block Lee's troops had they retreated south from Virginia. Wrecking and burning as they traveled, they targeted Salisbury, an important Rebel supply point, where they drove off Confederate troops and torched the town.[34] News of the surrender reached them as they fulfilled the ordered raids, the same as with those in December, accomplishing what was expected. They traveled for a month, returning to Knoxville at the end of April. For Keogh and Stoneman, the Civil War was then over for them, as well.

In all, more than 620,000 Americans died in the Civil War, twice as many from disease than those lost in battle. Fifty thousand came home as amputees. On December 6, 1865 the Thirteenth Amendment to the U.S. Constitution was ratified, becoming the law of the land. Slavery was abolished.

TAKING LEAVE IN THE END OF MAY, KEOGH MADE A DIFFICULT TRIP

to Washington. Joseph O'Keefe, his friend since their soldiering days in Italy, was a patient at Providence Hospital in the Capitol, succumbing to complications from old and new battle wounds. He had been wounded at the Battle of Brandy Station, but recuperated to serve with Sheridan. Fighting with his forces at Five Forks, Virginia, on April 1, O'Keefe was struck three times, one bullet shattering his right knee. He died on May 30, 1865 with Keogh by his bedside.[35]

It was a sad time but, also, apparently a happy one. Keogh, according to the story that came to light later, was in love. He was a very attractive man and, as many snippets of information suggest, had an eye for the ladies. But at the same time, he was totally circumspect and revealed almost nothing about his personal affairs. Still, in a letter to his brother, Tom, he hinted at the entanglements and complications presented by a romantic relationship.

"I have had plenty of trials and have them still," he said, adding, "... my great weakness is the love I have for the fair sex & pretty much all my troubles come or can be traced to that charming source."[36] For many soldiers, military life was a family affair, wives frequently showing up in camp between battle engagements and creating, as much as possible, a home-like atmosphere. But Keogh seemed reluctant to even consider it, describing himself as "to [sic] proud to marry and have my wife support herself," though he thought that an economical wife might make it work out well.[37]

If such thoughts occupied his mind, so did more ambitious ones. With war over, the Union volunteer army was slated to be disbanded, and with that he would lose his rank as captain and position with Stoneman. He had gathered several glowing recommendations from commanders he had served directly and others who had seen his performance at close range, and he was hopeful he could parlay them into a permanent commission in the regular U.S. Army.

Added to what McClellan had said, and what Stoneman had told Sheridan, General Jacob Cox, who had fought at Antietam and in the Atlanta Campaign , described "... no officer of his grade who made [a] more enviable reputation, or proved more conclusively that he was born a soldier."[38] Schofield, who had brought Stoneman and Keogh to the Western Theater, said simply, "He is one of the most gallant and efficient young cavalry officers I have ever known."[39]

Keogh continued with Stoneman, now commander of the Department of Tennessee, for the next 18 months. They were in Memphis on a completely new assignment, the massive challenge of Reconstruction. As the U.S. government implemented a program designed to bring the seceded states back into the Union, on the local level Keogh and Stoneman's other officers put down riots, in other ways defused racial tensions, and worked to maintain the peace.

The process by which the seceded Southern states could rejoin the Union began a month after the war ended, with the U.S. Army being called to do what it had never done before, and that was to occupy rebellious states in peacetime. Thereupon, in a patchwork of leaders' visions and plans, implemented by the Federal and state governments, the eleven states followed procedures to reject their former Confederate positions and restore their places within the United States of America.

Reconstruction officially lasted 12 years, from 1865 to 1877. It was an immense and complicated undertaking, fraught with problems at all levels. The Civil War had settled two issues, the abolition of slavery, and the restoration of the Union. What had not been addressed were the civil, political, and economic rights of former slaves or freedmen, among other issues.

The Federal government established mechanisms for states to follow, that would grant them reentry in good standing. But at ground level, the U.S. Army moved quickly into the 11 states, now divided into military districts, to keep the peace the best they knew how. The South's economy had been destroyed, its railroads, heavy industries, and manufacturing wrecked in the final months of the war. A rapid economic rebound was an impossibility, leaving people financially ruined and bitter. Their anger spilled out, against blacks, Northerners, local Union supporters, and other targets. Tensions ran high, crowds were hard to control. Blacks were assaulted and killed in high numbers, in individual crimes and en masse, sometimes including whites who tried to help. Hate groups grew, led by the Ku Klux Klan.

Keogh and his colleagues tackled assignments that were a microcosm of what happened in cities and towns across the South. For Stoneman, the duties were complicated by the fact that he had only 150 soldiers available, a typical situation for the occupying army as the volunteer cavalry regiments were disbanded.[40] On two nights in May 1866, as his men attempted to control a white mob marauding through the black neighborhood called South Memphis, Stoneman was finally forced to declare martial law to restore order.[41]

Reconstruction succeeded in its primary goal of bringing the former Confederate states back to the Union. But the larger, more diffuse challenges, namely to help the South come to grips with a new reality, took far longer. Perhaps Sherman said it best, that "no matter what change we may desire in the feelings and thoughts of the people [in the] South, we cannot accomplish it by force."[42]

YET, EVEN WITH THE ABRUPT CHANGE FROM WARTIME TO OCCUPATION, it was a pleasant time for Keogh. Mixed in with his military duties were chances to renew friendships with former comrades and start new ones. Still, true to form, the soldier was ready for something more. He was looking for his next challenge, and he had some ideas. At the end of 1866, Keogh gave Stoneman his notice, resigning his post. The U.S. Army was forming new cavalry regiments, and he wanted in.

Chapter 5

SECURING THE FRONTIER

In the summer of 1866, Myles Keogh had what he wanted and what he had worked hard to achieve, a commission in the regular U.S. Army. As of July 26, he was officially a captain in the newly formed U.S. 7th Cavalry, and he was now on his way to Fort Riley, where the regiment was mustered in. He headed west from bustling Washington, across states of the Midwest, the mighty Mississippi and the wide Missouri, to the endless open plains of frontier Kansas.

Where Keogh was going was a complete change from anything he was used to, likely more than he could have imagined. Kansas was a new state, entering the Union five years earlier, just months before the Civil War broke out. The nearest town to Fort Riley, five miles to the south, had only been settled in 1854, and then it took a few name changes before Junction City stuck.[1] The Kansas Pacific Railroad, eventually to link Kansas City with Denver, Colorado, conveniently had reached Junction City in June[2], so Keogh had only a short stage-coach ride from the railroad station in town to the fort.

The competition for the commission he had sought had been stiff, 500 men applying for only 12 captain slots.[3] But the impression

Keogh had made on many commanders during the Civil War had clearly elevated his chances, a number of them sending individual letters, together with a joint request from all going directly to President Johnson.[4]

As he had considered his future, Keogh was clear-eyed about how vital such recommendations were, especially for someone who had not attended a military academy or, as a foreigner, didn't have a congressman who could promote him. As a captain, he told his brother, Tom, he would be working with distinguished senior commanders, adding, "This is for one of my age almost unprecedented in the regular army..."[5]

The outcome reversed a brief disappointment, quite possibly thanks to the support from the commanders who wanted to see Keogh's talents better used. Initially, he had been given the commission of second lieutenant in the 4th Cavalry, a rank clearly below what he hoped for. But before he could pack his bags and leave Washington, those orders were rescinded and new ones directed Captain Keogh to Fort Riley.

Whether Tom was surprised that his younger brother would be staying in the U.S., or given the streak of wanderlust that Myles had shown, at least from the time he left for Italy, that this was something he rather expected, is debatable. Tom appeared to be the settled brother, the family anchor, one might say. He would marry and move away from their home, Orchard House, but just to a neighboring town. He was Myles' touchstone, and in a Christmas letter of 1865, his young brother told Tom of his decision, describing America as, "a great country for a man of intellect, energy and capital," where he "expected to be much better off than he could hope to be, even under the most favourable [sic] circumstances in Ireland."[6]

In the 1860s, Kansas, particularly the western part, still was considered part of the frontier, the forefront of settlements growing in the state. It was a moving line that inched forward as people flooded into Kansas and elsewhere, pushing ever west and challenging the Indians to give up their land. As the Indians fought back, their uprisings increasing, the U.S. Army moved in to protect the settlers, the railroad workers laying tracks across an area, and the stagecoaches rolling through. It had been this way before the Civil War, when members of the cavalry and the infantry were spread across the West, fighting Indians all the way to California and the Northwest. Now they were all back at it, fighting harder for the land that both sides desperately wanted, but this time the cavalry was at the center. No longer was it the force that fought for recognition, as it did through the Civil War, from peripheral use at the beginning to the point of greater acceptance as mounted fighters by the end. In the west, the cavalry was king.

Most of the officers in the Civil War, on both sides, had previous experience fighting the Indians. Stoneman was a noted Indian fighter in California and Oregon, and later on frontier duty in Texas.[7] Sheridan, Stoneman, and Shields all served in the Mexican War, and Sheridan also fought Indians in California and the Northwest. Southern-born Gillem was on the front lines during the Third Seminole War in Florida, and thereafter on the Texas frontier.

Buford, riding with the cavalry from the time he graduated from West Point, with both the First and then the Second U.S. Dragoons, served on frontier duty around the west.[8] Listening to those men, officers who Keogh respected, talk of the West they knew, gave him a good sense of the frontier situation and helped him make his decision, to sign on to be a frontier cavalryman.

As the Civil War intensified, regular army units garrisoned at forts across the west were pulled off their posts and sent east to fight for the North and South. In their place, state militias moved into the breach, functioning as best they could to continue protecting the locals. But when the volunteer army disbanded in 1866, the militias ceded the job back to the U.S. Cavalry, now ten regiments, an increase of four immediately following the Civil War. Informally known as the Plains Cavalry, this period in its history and its role of protecting the frontier actually lasted well into the 1890s.

Among the regiments, the 7th Cavalry had a certain aura, a presence if you will, that continued through the years. It was initially led by the highly regarded, ambitious, and flamboyant General George Armstrong Custer. He had served for the duration of the Civil War, a captain by commission who was brevetted to the rank of Brigadier General at age 23, and Major General at age 25, in both cases the youngest soldier ever to be brevetted to those levels.[9] From early in the war, he was applauded for his leadership and bravery, and by war's end commanded an entire cavalry division.

What he and Keogh felt about each other, from their brief association in the Civil War, is unknown. It doesn't seem that the relationship was anything more than cordial, but it is clear that Custer respected Keogh's abilities and wanted him on his team. In a letter to his wife, Libbie, Custer commented that he "...would rather have him near us than many others."[10]

At very least, Keogh was proud of his appointment, this time the personal connection being less of an issue than the position he had attained, commander of Company I of the 7th Cavalry. He was Custer's fourth senior captain and would ride with him thereafter, in due course becoming his commander's most senior officer.

MOST OF THE WESTERN FORTS HAD SHORT LIVES. SEVERAL WERE attached to each regiment, those commissioned by the 7th Regiment built across Kansas and Colorado. Each fort was established as military protection in an area out of necessity, remained garrisoned until the danger had passed, and then was closed down and abandoned. Some forts survived in the condition they were left in, until many years later when they became historic landmarks. Others stood empty until locals stripped them of their building materials, log by log and board by board, until nothing was left and the fort quite literally disappeared. Such was the eventual fate of Fort Wallace, Keogh's command in its prime.

Fort Riley was luckier than that. Opened in 1853, for the first few months called Camp Center for its location at the approximate center of the country, it became the first home of the 7th Cavalry.[11] But even after it lost that tenant and, through the years, grew less important as populations pushed west, the fort stayed open. Finally in 1884, Sheridan, who late in his career became Chief of the Army, resurrected Fort Riley when he recommended to Congress that it become Cavalry Headquarters of the Army[12], the position it still holds today.

Keogh's arrival at Fort Riley in the late summer of 1866 was an interim stop on his way across Kansas to Fort Wallace, the antithesis of what he was leaving behind. Fort Riley was a large, organized establishment on the eastern, more settled side of Kansas, near Leavenworth and St. Louis, Missouri and other supply points. Fort Wallace was the complete opposite, a desolate spot some 270 miles west, on the banks of the Smoky Hill River at the edge of the frontier.

At age 26, Keogh would be the ranking officer and commander of the farthest west of any fort in the state. The Plains Indians were fighting fiercely against the encroaching settlers, and in the area around Fort Wallace hostilities were at their worst of anywhere in Kansas.[13]

The Butterfield Overland Despatch (BOD), the formal name for the new stagecoach that went along the Smoky Hill Trail, linked Atkinson, Kansas with Denver, Colorado, nearly 600 miles distant. There were stops every 15 miles or so, some to feed the travelers, others to hay and water the horses and mules. Although advertised as a way for travelers to cross the western plains in safety, the food stop close to Fort Wallace was the target of Indian attacks so often that the line lost business and eventually was sold. Indian trouble soon earned Wallace the title of the Fightin'est Fort in the West.[14]

AT FORT RILEY, KEOGH AND THE MEN WHO WOULD SERVE WITH HIM organized a wagon train to move themselves, their horses, and all the equipment and provisions they would need on the trip and as they began life at Fort Wallace. Given that just one company was headed to the fort, the caravan would have been moderate-sized compared to some others.

But the basic components were always the same: mounted troops, additional unsaddled horses, and heavily packed, mule-drawn wagons. The caravan's speed varied widely as they walked anywhere from 10 to 20 miles a day, depending on weather, terrain, breakdowns, and other problems. But taking a daily average of 15 miles, the trip across Kansas most likely took a month and maybe more.

It is doubtful that Keogh knew much if anything about the barely habitable situation that awaited him. Construction on Fort Wallace had begun in September of the previous year, but problems had slowed its completion and false reports to cavalry headquarters had minimized the extent of what still had to be done. Nevertheless, a few days before Thanksgiving 1866, as Keogh and his men of Company I of the U.S. 7th Cavalry rode onto the grounds of the fort, what they were going to deal with became shockingly clear.

The new commander should have found, had the building plan been completed as scheduled, a fort ready to provide comfortable living for a full garrison, a term that described a varying number of men in the hundreds. There were to be two buildings for cavalrymen and one for the infantry, a mess hall and kitchen, quarters and separate kitchens for two captains, a medical officer, and four lieutenants.

Plans also called for a guardhouse, stables for horses and other animals, and buildings for the carpenter, the wheelwright (who worked specifically on wheels), and the blacksmith, in addition to buildings for storage.[15]

What the arrivals found was very different! The situation regarding troop housing was abysmal. Of the three buildings planned, one did not even have its foundation laid, another was halfway completed, and the third, in need of a roof, was so badly constructed to that point that Keogh doubted that it could support even the lightest roof.[16] As well, the horse stalls had walls but no roofs.

If there was any bright spot at all, it was that many of Keogh's men, if untrained in the cavalry basics of horsemanship and weaponry (the same skills lacking in many recruits to the Civil War), came to the military with skills from their previous lives. They were carpenters, masons, and others skilled in the building trades, and they went to work making Fort Wallace, at very least, a functional place.

While the fort could accommodate several companies, a number that would equal its full garrison, rarely were there anywhere near that many soldiers in residence. Far more often, the average population was some 75 soldiers. Again, much like the Civil War, many were immigrants, mostly German and Irish, with other nationalities mixed in. They were drawn to the army for many of the same reasons as before, though probably less about patriotism than a chance to get out of poverty and start a new life. It was a job and a steady (if modest) paycheck, and for many it was a chance to get away from the widespread prejudice toward immigrants.

A soldier's beginning pay was $16.00 a month, reduced by one dollar for savings, and 12-1/2 cents for the Soldiers Home (of which there were several), giving him a net pay of $14.87 and a half cents per month[17] for what was hazardous, sometimes fatal duty.

Nor were the threats only from the Indians. Disease took its toll, mostly from dysentery and diarrhea, and outbreaks of cholera. For some, the negatives were far too many and they deserted.

There were those who looked upon the cavalry as an American

version of the French Foreign Legion, a place to lose yourself (or find yourself, as the case might be), and where few questions were asked. On occasion, it has even been suggested that Keogh, himself, fought with the Legion, though an examination of the Legion's history alongside that of Keogh's would make his service with the Legion virtually impossible.

The Legion fought in Algeria in 1850, when Keogh was ten years old, and in northern Italy in 1859, the year before he left Ireland to fight in the Papal War. Certainly, joining the French Foreign Legion could have been an intoxicating idea for a young man as anxious to get on with his life as Keogh appeared to be. One could fight under an assumed name, and Keogh might even have suggested to some people that he joined. But for the young man who was known for his integrity by so many during the Civil War, it would be hard to believe that Keogh would actually make such a serious declaration as having served with the Legion.

MEANWHILE AT FORT WALLACE THE PROBLEMS MULTIPLIED. IT WAS almost winter when they arrived, and on the western plains of Kansas it was already very cold. The men worked as rapidly as they could to build housing but, for the immediate future, the men were forced to live in unheated tents, given that the heating stoves had arrived, but not the stove pipes. Worse, in a snowy environment, the horses that had just endured the long trek across the state, had to survive virtually in the open. Whatever stall walls existed plus available blanketing would have been the extent of protection from wind and snow.

As weather permitted, the same men who were building the fort also needed to learn how to ride a horse in combat. Some had never sat on a horse before they walked one across Kansas with the wagon train, others knew how to ride, perhaps very well. But fighting Indians took new and different skills. It often meant a high-speed chase, holding the reins in one hand while firing a weapon with the other, not to mention controlling your horse in what could be a tumultuous situation filled with noise, smoke, and dead riders and horses hitting the ground.

The men quickly learned the importance of their horses as trusted combat partners, and how to care for them diligently and twice a day. Meanwhile, Indian attacks were expected to escalate, demanding of the men what we would call today on the job training, as drills and chasing Indians would frequently occur on the same day.

Adding to the difficulties at the fort itself that first winter, 1866-67, was a notification from district headquarters containing a serious warning. Indian hostilities were clearly going to ramp up, and Fort Wallace would be strategically more important than ever.[18] The warning was borne out. Between the end of April and mid-June 1867, Indians attacked the Butterfield Overland stagecoach 27 times while it was on route. Keogh, a militarist who was trained in the more cohesive tactics of western warfare, was frustrated in the extreme. Fighting Indians, he found out very quickly, was very different from everything he had been used to in Italy and the Civil War.

The Indians would swoop down on their target, run off the horses, torch the hay and buildings, and cause other mayhem, and then gallop off, disappearing into their territory with the speed and nimbleness that left the cavalrymen in their dust, helpless to find and capture their attackers. Finally, after a string of raids and fruitless attempts to bring in any Indian captives, Keogh's disgust at the defensive approach his men were forced to take boiled over and he fired off a letter to Regimental Adjutant Myles Moylan:

> It is ridiculous to expect me to protect the different stations unless I close up the post and divide the garrison between Willow Creek and Monument Station [two stagecoach stops]. If the Indians are not followed up to their village and killed, then it is useless to expect peace or rest on this route.[19]

The captain was not one to suffer fools lightly, but neither was the U.S. Cavalry quick to bend and change their ways. Keogh's sharp tongue was not appreciated, and the only thing his frustration got him was a reprimand from district headquarters. The captain had repeatedly requested more troop assistance. As well, it did nothing to damp down his anger that construction on the fort, which had been progressing, ground to a halt in the summer. Lumber from Denver could not be delivered because Indian presence made the road unsafe, and Keogh could not spare troops which were needed to guard the fort and the stagecoach stops to escort the delivery.[20]

IN A BITTERSWEET WAY, THE CHALLENGES OF FORT WALLACE WERE an antidote for Keogh. He was always resolutely taciturn about his love life, but in bits and pieces written to his brother, Tom, he revealed a broken heart. Little of the story ever came from Keogh, but others reconstructed what is likely the timeline and synopsis of the romance from those letters. At the center was Abby Grace Clary, a young widow who Keogh probably met in 1865 when he was first on Reconstruction duty in Tennessee.

Abby had been married to Robert Emmett Clary, Jr., a captain in Buford's cavalry who Keogh surely would have known. Clary was a troubled young man who battled alcoholism, and who had been court-martialed three times because of drunken behavior and, finally, was dismissed from military service at the beginning of 1864.[21] Whether alcoholism played a part in his death, directly or indirectly, is unknown, but Clary died in December 1864 in Memphis.

Unfortunately, we don't know anything of the happy times, but given that Keogh had hoped to spend his life with Abby, there would have been many of them in the year and a half that they were together. But his plans were dashed when Abby, at age 28, suddenly died in mid-June 1866, the cause listed as gastro fever. It is thought that the term referred to appendicitis, a condition that was little understood and fatal in those years.

Keogh was out of town at the time, assigned to jury duty in Nashville, and returned a week after Abby's death to the heartbreaking news.[22]

Nevertheless, faced with moving beyond his personal feelings as he prepared for his journey to Fort Riley, it wasn't until August that the very private Keogh revealed anything of his sadness, even to his brother. Then his feelings came forth, a few lines at a time, over several letters. In August he acknowledged "how very, very lonely" he was. "I have had some things to try me severely so much so that the future is a matter of little importance to me so long as you all are comfortable ... I now have no one else to care for."[23]

Following in late October, Keogh was more forthcoming when he said to Tom,

> Now that my hopes are dead for my future earthly happiness & the dear creature I dreamt of being happy with lies yonder in Oakhill Cemetery where I have just visited her cold vault—I wish to tell you that I will devote myself to helping you provide for my darling sisters."[24] (Oakhill, in Georgetown, D.C., was where Clary's father-in-law had a plot.)

Of the three Keogh brothers, Myles was now the only bachelor, elder brother Patrick having married along with Tom. By the new year, he seemed more accepting of his situation, assuring Tom of his commitment to their family. "I will never marry," Keogh wrote then. "It may have been grief that changed me but changed I am & I seem to have only an idea that is for the happiness & comfort & above all the aggrandizement of my family."[25]

With their parents deceased, his generosity would benefit his unmarried sisters handsomely in providing their dowries, a very important part of what a young woman brought to marriage.

But, despite the melancholy that clouded those later months and beyond, it was the bright beginning of 1866 that would become a milestone in Keogh's life. In the spring, he traveled to Willowbrook, on the shores of Lake Owasco, near Auburn, New York, the first of several trips to visit his new friends, the Martin family. They were an old, established family in the area, a great uncle of what was originally the Throop-Martin family having been governor of New York State.

Stationed in Knoxville, at the start of his Reconstruction tour with Stoneman, Keogh had run into an old friend, General Andrew Alexander and his wife, Evy, and another couple, General Emory Upton and his fiancée, Evy's sister, Emily. The women were from the Martin family, and soon Keogh was invited to join them all at the Martin family estate. Over the next decade, they became very close, Evy Alexander saying of Keogh, "he wound himself about our hearts.[26] For his part, he basked in their affection, especially having the children call him, Uncle Keogh.[27]

Keogh, the Alexanders, and Upton shared a house in Knoxville, and it is possible that there he met a third Martin sister, Cornelia, known as "Nelly," when she visited Evy and Emily. Whether there or at Willowbrook, Keogh and Nelly developed a strong friendship. It has always been wondered, often presumed, that in time romance bloomed, but Keogh would never say. One thing is true, their connection remained close from their meeting through the remainder of both their lives.

KEOGH WAS A GOOD COMMANDER, TOUGH BUT FAIR, AND WELL LIKED by his men, whom he referred to in letters home to Ireland as "his boys."[28] His attitude was the same as it had been from his boyhood years in Ireland, that the horses be given the best care possible. The well being of the company's mounts was fundamental to what the cavalry did, and how well they did it, and Keogh was adamant that his men understand this. He also made sure that all understood that the man who didn't have a horse wound up a foot soldier. He was his own best example about how to treat horses, telling Tom:

> My horses are in excellent condition. I have had some hay cutting machines sent me and I mix the oats and hay. It is very fattening. We had eight hundred tons of hay put up here this fall [presumably 1867]. It costs 40 dollars per ton after being ricked [stacked] at the post.[29]

The captain had no patience for deserters, and when he caught up with one, he brought him back to the fort, docked his pay, and sent him to the brig. He also became creative, offering his men $30.00 for every deserter captured. Not surprisingly, his men became very adept at finding deserters, $30.00 being more than three months pay for a private.[30] His attitude was simple, his men didn't have to re-enlist, but during that first tour they didn't get to decide that cavalry life wasn't for them; they were expected to fulfill their responsibility.

True to fort life overall, what went on at Fort Wallace was a combination of repetitive, mundane days interspersed with adrenalin-pumping times when the Indians attacked. The daily routine started before sunrise with Keogh making rounds to see that everything was in order on base. Next came an hour of stable chores, then reveille and roll call. Hours of drills built rider confidence, after which more stable chores again catered to the needs of the horse. Before any man ate his dinner, his horse was rubbed down, watered, given his evening meal, and left with a pile of hay to munch.

But whether to survive the doldrums of routine days or calm the nerves after Indians attacked and galloped off, drinking in that environment could be a welcome pastime. Keogh indulged in and, at times it was said, did so heavily, though not once was the word, alcoholic, attached to his name.

Not surprisingly, however, his drinking opened him up to criticism, even if the stories that have survived have a questionable ring of truth. Among them was a report that Keogh, while making late rounds to check on the horses, heard some strange noises outside the stables, then roused the company to saddle up at midnight and ride out to investigate. The complainant, whoever he was, awakened to the sounds of the company moving out, then fell back asleep,[31] in a later report, scoffing at the legitimacy of a midnight raid and claiming Keogh was drunk. Did the accuser forget, or perhaps never knew, that the Indians liked to attack the fort at night, the easier to cause trouble and get away, and a prudent commander would take no chances?

Another complainant had just given up drinking himself, a state that apparently gave him license to look with disdain at all those who were still engaged in imbibing[32] of which, it should be noted, were many in the frontier cavalry. By contrast, Custer's wife, who chronicled much of that life and times in her several books, remembered Keogh differently, describing him, even when he overindulged of an evening, as a benign and delightful drunk, who was willing to let his striker care for him, and who broke into song at the drop of a hat.[33]

Keogh did, however, walk a fine line between his own occasional self indulgence and the need to be a stickler where his men were concerned, aware that too much drinking could affect the operation of the fort. He had succeeded in stopping the sale of liquor around Fort Wallace, but became concerned that it was going to be available at the Pond Creek Station. It was the nearest stagecoach stop to the fort, and Keogh knew full well that it would be an easy enough trip for the men to make.[34]

Nevertheless, Keogh, a caring commander, made sure that his boys had a proper and festive Christmas dinner in 1867, their second and more settled holiday at the fort. The feast that day included two fine antelopes, killed by the commander, and 10 gallons of Scotch whisky he ordered for the celebration, "much to the satisfaction of the Irish," he later told his family.[35]

It wasn't just for holidays, either. Keogh hunted whenever he had free time, proud of being a crack marksman who, so it was said, could shatter a bottle at 150 yards.[36] The fresh game he brought back gave his men better meals than the limited items in the larder, the likes of hash and long-cooked stew (the better to mask the taste of tainted meat), baked beans, coarse bread, salt bacon, the rock solid biscuit known as hardtack, that had to be soaked in liquid to be chewable, and coffee. The horses, not so fussy, thought hardtack was a treat without it being soaked.

WHAT EVERYONE SEEMED TO UNDERSTAND, CHAMPIONS AND detractors alike, was that whatever the truth of Keogh's drinking, it never interfered with his professionalism, nor his relationship with the men in his command, who remembered "that every man in his troop idolized him," and that he was "a good-hearted officer ... and a nice man."[37] Perhaps even more telling, his men reenlisted to continue serving with him, which says volumes about Keogh and his character.[38]

But much more than enjoying a convivial sing-a-long, as he was known to do, Keogh was a man who loved music and encouraged its enjoyment at Fort Wallace. Indeed, it is not farfetched to believe that the Irish among the men of Company I sang the rollicking Irish air, *Garryowen*, that would become the marching song of the 7th Cavalry. Some would surely have remembered the song, an old and popular military song, from their hometown pubs.

It was so widely known that a few years later, when it came to naming an official marching song for the 7th, any number of men could have suggested it. Nevertheless, Keogh may have been the one who made the suggestion to Custer, pleased that a song from the old country was being carried forth.

Garryowen, it is said, first gained popularity at a tavern in Limerick, Ireland, a watering hole for the Fifth Royal Irish Lancers, a unit stationed in the area. The name translates from the Gaelic words for Garden of Owen,[39] its popularity apparently growing in the American

Revolution, with the Irish Brigade in the Papal Wars, and then with any number of Irishmen who came to fight in our Civil War and beyond. Custer put his stamp of approval on it in 1867, as the regiment's official air. Thereafter, when troops rode out of the fort, two by two in a long blue line, the horses cantered to the music's brisk two-step beat. Though they might be riding toward danger, *Garryowen* sent the cavalry onward with pride.

1

Capt. Myles Keogh, in an 1862 photo, joined Union forces that year, then fought to war's end in more than 80 battles.

2

Keogh grew up in Leighlinbridge on Ireland's River Barrow. His family raised barley, which went downriver to the mills.

3

Brig. Gen. James Shields, Union commander in the Shenandoah Valley Campaign, gave Keogh his first staff appointment.

4

Gen. George McClellan, impressed with the young captain, shifted him from General Buford's staff to his own.

5

With Gen. George Stoneman, Keogh moved from the Eastern Theater to fight in the west and south.

6

Gen. George Custer knew Keogh from the Civil War, and wanted him as one of his officers in the 7th Cavalry.

7

Capt. Keogh wore his Papal medals on his chest or around his neck. At the Last Stand, one may have been his talisman.

8

Gen. John Buford, seated, with his staff officers. Keogh, left, and Buford became very close, like father and son.

9

An 1875 hunting party with 7th Cavalry officers and their ladies. Keogh is center left with Custer beside him.

10

Another social gathering of the 7th Cavalry, at Fort Abraham Lincoln. Keogh, center, reclines on the lowest step.

11

By fall 1876, Comanche, with Gustave Korn, was recovering well from battle wounds. Shown at Fort Lincoln, other horses are resting.

12

In 1879, the 7th Cavalry erected a monument to Keogh and the members of Company I at the Little Bighorn battlefield.

 13

Postcard celebrating Comanche's survival Comanche's fame led to a carte de visite with the legend, "The only animal that ever came out of the Custer massacre alive."

14 

Gen. Samuel Sturgis made Comanche the 7th Cavalry's 2nd Commanding Officer after the Little Bighorn.

 15

Prof. Lewis Dyche, famed taxidermist, took Comanche to the Chicago World Exposition, then home to Kansas.

16

Museum restorer Terry Brown gave Comanche a new lease on life in 2005.

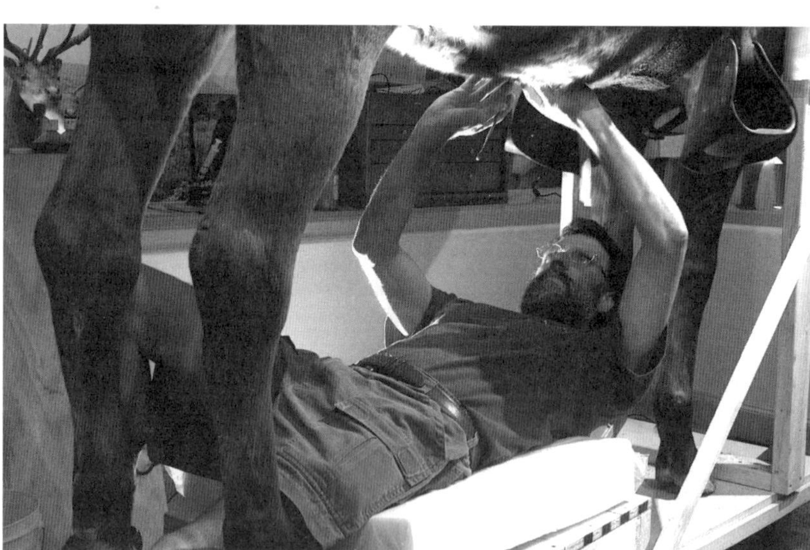
17

The university built a glass and plywood studio for Brown, so that people could watch from outside as he restored the famed horse.

18

Brown, his work completed, with Comanche.

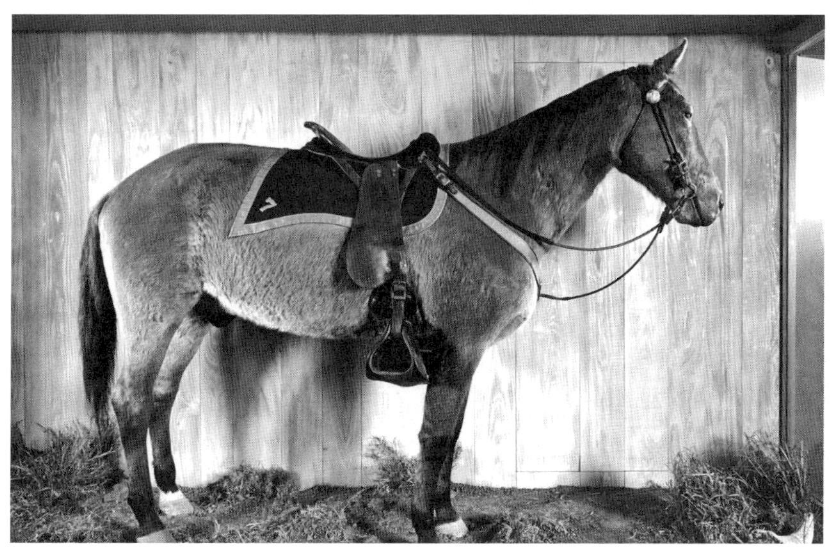

19

Comanche today, a popular stop on the main floor of the Museum of Natural History.

Chapter 6

A PARTNERSHIP BEGINS

After his equine partner, Tom, died in the summer of 1864, Keogh never talked of another horse. There were no letters to his brother and sister, brimming with pride about a new mount, the talents he was showing, and the special care Keogh was giving him. The captain was riding horses, of that there was no question. He was a cavalryman, after all, and horses were part of his life. Indeed, once he had joined the 7th Cavalry and moved Company I to Fort Wallace, horses were vital to what they were doing there. Hours of every day Keogh would have spent in the saddle, riding and training horses, teaching and drilling his men. Still, there never seemed to be that special one, one he wanted to tell others about. But then, four years after he lost Tom, another one finally came along, elevated to that singular place. His name was Comanche.

He first showed up in the spring of 1868, one in a herd of horses delivered by a horse trader to a holding depot in St. Louis. The traders were called mustangers, men mostly working in what was variously called the Wild Horse Desert or Great Horse Desert of Texas, a huge stretch of land in south Texas between the Rio Grande River at its south edge, and the Nueces River farther north. There they wrangled colts out of the wild horse herds, castrated them, and shipped them north, just like they did the cattle herds, to where the horses could be purchased by officers for the needs of their individual regiments. It was run as a contract system by the U.S. Army Quartermaster Department, an arrangement that started after the close of the Cavalry Bureau, with its massive horse depots that supplied the Union Army in the latter days of the Civil War. Although quality control and corruption were ongoing problems of the contract system, the eventual solution, the U.S. Army Remount Program with its massive purchasing and breeding operations, didn't come into being until more than 40 years later.[1]

On April 3, 1868, a group of 40 (perhaps 41) horses, a mix of mustangs and cross-breeds being temporarily corralled in St. Louis, found a prospective buyer. The 7th Cavalry was in the market to replenish horses lost over the previous winter and took the group on consignment. Packed into railroad cars, they were sent across Missouri to Fort Leavenworth, on the east edge of Kansas just north of Kansas City.

Unsettling as all the moving around would have been to the horses, Fort Leavenworth was a giant step up from the vile holding pens of St. Louis. Nothing good could be said of this situation, other than any horse that survived was reasonably tough and likely made tougher by not succumbing to the squalor. The jammed pens were filled with the horses' feces, in warm weather their bodies blanketed by swarms of flies. Their nourishment came from troughs of stagnant water and hay tossed into the muck. The result was a sad story of injury and disease killing many horses before they could be sold.

With its equine-centered history as home of the First and Second U.S. Dragoons (later reorganized as cavalry regiments), Fort Leavenworth was a logical place for potential buyers to size up the prospects. Lieutenant Tom Custer, younger brother of the 7th Cavalry's commander, had come to do just that, examine the shipment just arrived before finalizing the order. The average price paid by the U.S. Army for each horse was $90.00, comparable today to a little over $1,500.00,[2] a negotiable amount based on the animal's conformation, suitability, and its basic level of training. Custer's brother found the group to be in good shape, after which each was branded with "US" on the left shoulder and "C" on the left thigh. The cavalry number was sometimes added on the thigh, sometimes not. The horses had now moved onto the U.S. government payroll, to be fed, shod, and in all other ways cared for to the best of the 7th Cavalry's ability.

AT WHAT POINT THE HORSE, WHO WOULD SOON BEAR THE NAME Comanche, emerged from the pack to be an animal of note is swathed in stories. His statistics were listed, likely on a bill of sale presented to Custer for his signature. The horse was said to be six years old, making his date of birth 1862, the same year that Keogh arrived in the U.S., entered the Civil War and, it could rightly be noted, began his American adventure. For those who appreciate connection, the last could also be said of Comanche.

He was recorded at 15 hands (an equine measure equaling five feet) at the withers, the point at which the neck and back meet, and he was estimated to be about 925 pounds, likely in need of a little more weight after the stress of his trip north. The phrase used to describe him was, "nicely put up,"[3] suggesting a well-proportioned and balanced horse, clean-legged with a strong back, and whose overall appearance was solid, sturdy, and pleasing. His color was called claybank, in appearance a light golden brown coat with a blonde undercoat, the undertone visible by itself on his belly. Importantly, a claybank's points—the mane, tail and legs—are not black but a darker tone of the coat, in Comanche's case, an oak brown, the legs lighter than the mane and tail. He stood out, a horse to be noticed.

LOADED BACK INTO RAILROAD CARS, THE 7TH CAVALRY'S NEWEST

members headed farther west, 300 miles from Fort Leavenworth to Ellis Station, where the cavalry was encamped. It was mid-May 1868 and the horses were about to begin basic training at nearby Fort Hays, another of the regiment's forts near the Smokey Hills River. For these new mounts, gone was the life of the desert, the freedom of movement mixed with the challenges of finding food and water, and the often dire consequences of untended injuries. Instead, as cavalry horses they must accept the sounds of drums, bugles, and bands, and the feel of bit and bridle, the dig of spurs, and the weight of saddle and rider, frequently for long stretches at a time. It was a regimented life, also harsh, but now with plentiful food, clean water, and shelter from the elements.

Just when the handsome claybank Mustang and Keogh became partners is open to debate, and not a little creativity (beginning with some belief that he was a Mustang-Morgan mix, a contention not supported by early U.S. Army records). That Keogh, generally acknowledged to be in need of a horse to replace one recently killed, was drawn to Comanche in a ring at Fort Hays is certainly an engaging picture, and not without possibility. The story goes that Comanche was in a corral with other horses and Keogh, from the other side of the fence, locked eyes with him. Then beckoning him forward, Keogh was impressed that the horse came right to him. Comanche's boldness, it is said, essentially sealed the deal and Keogh purchased him for himself.[4]

A much different story, one we know to be accurate in terms of cavalry operations, had Keogh fighting Indians in September 1868 in Indian Territory (now Oklahoma), with Colonel Alfred Sully and several companies of the 7th and 3rd cavalries. Keogh had been drafted by Sully earlier to serve as an inspector general, charged with surveying posts and forts throughout Colorado and south to the New Mexico border. Now, again riding with Sully, they moved out from Fort Dodge, some one hundred miles due south of Fort Hayes. Their targets were Indians between the Cimarron and Arkansas rivers, west of present-day Tulsa, from whom they were after payback for Indian raids throughout Kansas the summer before.[5]

Sending Keogh on assignment away from Fort Wallace, thus leaving staff officers to deal with problems that arose around home base, was an example of the peripatetic nature of cavalry life in which commanders and companies were frequently moved. During this particular fight, facing the fearsome warriors, the Comanches, along with Kiowas and Cheyennes, Keogh's horse was shot out from under him and he called for a replacement from the pack.[6] The new horse, proving himself a tough campaigner became, in short order, Keogh's Comanche.

What most historians agree upon is that in battle, either the aforementioned fight or another, Comanche was struck in his rump by an arrow. His reaction was so stoic that Keogh admitted later to not realizing his horse had been hit, only remembering a whirring noise as the arrow pierced the flesh. Some say Comanche yelled when struck, a sound swallowed by the cacophony of Indian yells filling the air. Others say he yelled that night when, back at camp, the company farrier was extracting the arrow. Whatever the story, the core truth is that Keogh was very impressed with this new horse, one that he was convinced was sound of body and mind. Evocative of the drama of his early years, and his toughness against the best of the Indian fighters, he would be called Comanche.

EACH CAVALRY OFFICER HAD TWO HORSES, ONE OR BOTH OF WHICH could belong to the U.S. government or, should the officer choose, be his personal property. In that case, the officer could handle the acquisition privately, or choose one from the regiment's herd of government horses, which were sold at the same price as the military paid the original horse trader. Thus, Comanche came to Keogh for $90.00. Beyond that initial outlay, given that the horse worked for the cavalry, the government paid all his other expenses, including food, upkeep, and whatever else arose. Still, Keogh was known to buy special feed not just for Comanche but all the horses in his care, at his own expense.[7]

Throughout Keogh's military career, Comanche was the only horse that he purchased. It was an unusual union, the polished, elegant captain and horseman, and a horse as tough and unflinching as the harsh land from which he came. From the time Keogh enlisted to fight in the Civil War, always as a member of the officer ranks, he moved among people with connections. When he was ready to own, he could have had whatever horse he wanted. Any of the sleek Eastern breeds would have been an easy choice, flashy speed horses like Custer's thoroughbreds, Vic (for Victory) or Dandy, or Ulysses Grant's Cincinnati, an American Saddlebred like Robert E. Lee's Traveller, or even a fine Morgan from New England.

But his instincts told him differently. To him, the better choice was the one from the unforgiving desert, who survived and prospered there. Keogh would ride the powerful, young Mustang, his gut feelings telling him this was the horse who could serve him best. He would train him further, to his exacting likes and needs, never to be ridden by a lesser horseman who, unwittingly, could undo what Keogh had instilled.

Comanche was his special horse, his warhorse, saved for long marches and battles, able to deliver that extra level of performance when it was needed. In Keogh's absence, he would have been cared for as if his master was there, and exercised only by someone of Keogh's choosing. Not to worry, Paddy, his second horse, suffered no slight. He, too, was Keogh's charge, given love and the best of care, just as Comanche was. Paddy never moved into the ranks of private horses, instead spending his life owned by the U.S. government. But he was part of the team of Keogh, Comanche and Paddy.

BY THE NUMBERS, THE FRONTIER CAVALRIES HAD A BIG APPETITE, NOT just for horses but also for mules and oxen. They were not as great as the numbers that sapped the South and the Union, of horse stock. But the needs of ten cavalry regiments were still demanding. The count for June 30, 1868, of the total four-legged population in service to the U.S. Army was 9,433 cavalry horses, 749 horses specifically to haul artillery, 17,866 mules and 211 oxen to pull components of the wagon trains, and 1,808 horses reserved for officers' use.

But the quantities of both horses and mules was only part of what the cavalries required. The horses themselves, often moving at sustained high speeds and for long distances with the cavalry, needed more food than their counterparts in the Civil War, or those acquired from other occupations. With the high energy cavalry mounts put forth, often for hours on end, they needed on average 12 pounds of hay or 14 pounds of grain,[8] or a comparable mix per day. Spread out across many western posts, as these animals were, supplying their food of necessity became the responsibility of the individual fort. Grain was purchased from the nearest markets, while the first choice for hay was for members of the fort's garrison to plant and harvest it themselves. Some posts even acquired mowing machines, which made it easier to keep the cost of hay down.[9] Overall for the cavalrymen, harvesting what they could, and buying from local farmers produced a workable arrangement.

At home base, the cavalry's horses ate at the same time each day, but on the trail it was a different matter. The reality of being away was that food and water were not always available, and the best horses could maintain a constant level of energy without it. On runs, be they patrols or actually giving chase to harassing Indians, the anticipated length of the trip dictated what the horses could expect. For short sorties, sometimes called hot chases, they didn't get to eat, though on longer runs, riders might stop on the return trip to allow them to graze. Water came from a local stream, when found. Once back at the fort, after a good rubdown, the horses got their dinner.

But when the cavalry set out on longer trips, carrying the fight to more distant trouble spots, the operation grew much larger. Traveling hundreds of miles, as was the case when Keogh rode with Sully and several companies of cavalrymen to fight in Indian Territory, a wagon train was essential. By 1867 the Army had established a Pack Train Service, run out of Camp Carlin near Cheyenne, Wyoming, from which a team of men and mules could report to a fort to handle all aspects of the train from packing to moving it to its destination.[10] Whether or not Sully chose to use the service is not known, as the choice was up to the commander and many preferred to have their own men handle the job. Either way, wagon trains (also called pack trains or supply trains) were the only way to feed and otherwise supply men and horses in the field.

All breeds had their proponents and detractors, but it was hard to dismiss the Mustang's ability to go long hours with minimal or no food and drink, a trait borne of their desert beginnings. They migrated first from the Middle East to North Africa, and then via the Moorish invasion to Spain. They were the horses of the Conquistadors, professional mercenaries who conquered lands around the world for Spain and Portugal. Their horses were light, fast, smart, and trainable, about 14 hands, and bred to live off the plains of Spain, eat grasses, go long distances without water, and forage in winter.[11] When explorers brought their horses to Mexico in the late 16th and17th centuries, then left them when they returned to Europe, they prospered, seeding the great mustang herds that traveled north to the southwestern U.S. Most stayed there on lands similar to their historic homelands of Spain and Mexico. But others kept moving, west to California, and northward, some as far as the southern tier of Canada, notably the western provinces of Alberta and Saskatchewan. Those that headed into the mountains of Colorado, Wyoming, and beyond, developed a hardiness to colder climes, valuable to buyers in those areas, and like their southern brothers, were wrangled off the land, broke, and sent to market.

Years before Comanche, Mustang numbers were immense, estimates in the southwest ranging in the millions. After traveling in the Wild Horse Desert in 1846, Grant wrote in his memoirs that he wondered if the numbers he saw could even fit into Rhode Island or Delaware.[12] But within a few years, those numbers had dropped dramatically, the result of being hunted like the buffalo, and captured by intrepid local herders who sold to cowboys, ranchers, and the U.S. Army.

The methods of capture were rough, often brutal, from creasing, to corralling and walking down. Creasing required a crack shot to send a bullet into the top line of the horse's neck, grazing the cartilage above the neck bones. The hit would stun and drop the horse, and mustangers would move in to put a halter on and hobble his legs, so that when he awoke he was unable to get away. It was a dicey maneuver with a narrow range of outcomes, its success dependent on the perfect shot. Anything other than that likely killed the horse instantly or mortally wounded him, or to his good fortune, missed him entirely. But with millions of wild horses available, killing some hardly mattered. Fortunately, Westerners had little stomach for creasing, and it is said that it was done far less than its notoriety suggested. Far more acceptable was running a horse into a makeshift corral, then lassoing him and working him down to some level of obedience, or separating a horse from the herd and keeping him moving constantly until, out of utter fatigue, he submitted to a rope tied around his neck.[13]

INJURIES WHILE ON ASSIGNMENT WERE PART OF THE JOB FOR THE cavalry horses, and Comanche endured his fair share. There were three that we know of in his first few years with Keogh, beginning with the arrow in his rump that, given the grit with which he handled it, was what initially impressed the captain. Two years later, fighting Indians some distance east of Fort Wallace on the Saline River, Comanche took an arrow to a leg, this time sidelining him for a month until the injury healed. The next year, 1871, the pair left Indian fighting behind and headed to Kentucky, for Keogh a second round of Reconstruction duty, this time dealing with the trouble-making Ku Klux Klan, carpetbaggers, and moonshiners operating illegal distilleries. Frequently called upon to control crowds, on one assignment it led to Comanche sustaining a wound to the right shoulder, this time presumably from a bullet, when a mob at one such distillery got unruly. What continued to impress Keogh each time was Comanche's willingness to push on, to ignore his injury and continue the fight.[14] Beyond attitude, he was sustained by the luck of inherently good health, the ability to heal well without complications, and the attention of a proud and loving owner. Comanche stepped up to the partnership at every turn.

Many horses were not so fortunate, the level of care then still very limited, mostly addressing the symptoms—cleaning a wound and keeping it cleaned, hoping it didn't get infected, and generally keeping the horse comfortable. Sometimes it was enough to save them, other times not. Post Civil War, more horses continued to die off the battlefield than on it. Still, for Comanche and other horses lucky enough to belong to lifelong horsemen, like Keogh, the breadth of what these men knew of horse care was often enough to keep their mounts in good form.

The concern for animals, and such attempts at veterinary medicine as were possible stretch far back, apparent by archaeological evidence in ancient Chinese, Egyptian, Babylonian, and Greek cultures. The Code of Hammurabi, authored by the Babylonian king (1792-1750 BCE), went so far as to carve in stone not only veterinary fees but also fines for malpractice. A thousand years later, Hippocrates laid the foundation for all medicine, veterinary and human, when he asserted that disease was not inflicted by the gods, but the doing of man through his environment, what he ate, and how he lived.[15]

However, people through time understood the perennial homage to farriers, "no hoof, no horse," and that it was those men who influenced the growth of veterinary medicine, by the Middle Ages expanding their work from horseshoeing to more generalized horse care. In a move to improve the treatment of horses in and around London, in 1356 the Lord Mayor of that city asked farriers working within a seven-mile radius of London to join together, with an eye to regulating and improving their services.[16]

The modern era of veterinary medicine, distinct from other disciplines, began in France in 1761 when the first recognized veterinary school was opened in Lyon, France by Claude Bourgelat. The impetus was not horses but the French cattle herds that had been destroyed by plague,[17] the findings still an undeniably important step as people grappled with the needs of agriculture, industry and the animals that serviced them.

Furthering the cause of animal welfare and the improved treatment of their sick numbers, England followed France's lead with the opening of the Odiham Agricultural Society 1783. It would be another half century for the discipline of veterinary medicine to become more targeted but in 1844, by royal charter, the Royal College of Veterinary Surgeons was founded.[18]

But changes on the ground came slowly. Still, early in the war, Lincoln's awareness of the dreadful treatment of horses, indeed the callous lack of it, set wheels in motion for their better future. In 1862, he signed the Morrill Act, popularly known as the Land-Grant College Act, which allowed states to sell large tracts of federal land and use the proceeds to establish colleges of agriculture and mechanical arts. Step by step, curricula were expanded to include courses in animal husbandry and veterinary practices and, eventually, independent colleges of veterinary medicine where chartered. Some of their graduates found their way to the cavalry, to provide better caliber veterinary practices there.

A year later, the civilian American Veterinary Medical Association was organized and began adding its muscle to the cause for a stronger veterinary presence in the military; the rapid result being the veterinary surgeon attached to each cavalry regiment. Significantly, instead of a draw-down in personnel after the Civil War ended, the four newly formed cavalry regiments were each given two veterinary surgeons, instead of the one assigned to the older cavalries. Unquestionably, the designated mounts and spare horses for the regiment's multiple companies was a heavy load even for two doctors, but post war it was progress. By 1881, those same surgeons were required to be graduates of legitimate veterinary schools or colleges.[19]

Seven years after it was organized at Fort Riley, in the fall of 1873 the 7th Cavalry shifted its headquarters north to the newly completed Fort Abraham Lincoln, ten miles south of Bismarck, North Dakota (then part of the Dakota Territory). Keogh and Comanche, with the rest of Company I, had just completed a tour at the Canadian border, serving as escorts for the Northern Border Survey team. The joint undertaking by the U.S. and Canada was, at that point, setting the portion of the border that stretched between Lake of the Woods, Minnesota and the summit of the Rocky Mountains.

Keogh reported to Fort Snelling, Minnesota, to wait for surveying to get underway, and while there bought himself a $10,000 life insurance policy. Some have attached a premonition to what he did, but in the summer of 1873 it seems more likely that, with some spare time on his hands, Keogh simply thought that it was a good idea. No doubt, a salesman from the New York Life Company,[20] who was apparently at the fort, encouraged the step. Keogh considered himself responsible for his sisters, and should the policy ever be paid out, it would benefit them. A number of his men must have shared his reasoning, because they also bought policies.

The cavalry had been spread out over the last couple of years, but now most companies were at headquarters. Indian activity across the center of the country was dying down, and the Army felt that the cavalry was needed in the Northern Plains where the Sioux and other tribes were still ready to fight any intrusions on their lands. It was an important move, militarily, but after more austere postings, such as Keogh's to Fort Wallace, the new fort was a welcome change.

Fort Abraham Lincoln was a village unto itself, a family-oriented community where the men could bring their wives and children to live. It was also one of the largest and most important forts on the Northern Plains.[21] It contained 78 separate buildings, including barracks for six companies of the 7th Cavalry and additional infantry companies, stabling for 600 horses, detached housing for officers, and log huts for Indian scouts, the latter two with room for family members. Its military importance notwithstanding, people at Fort Abraham Lincoln also enjoyed parties and dances, hunting trips, a billiard parlor, sleighing in winter, and entertainment by the enlisted men's Fort Lincoln Dramatic Association, that performed in the barracks theater.[22]

They were surely comfortable, even enjoyable days for Keogh, as he was remembered for often having "a wry smile for the ladies," they being the wives and female visitors to the fort. Other appealing details were his booming voice, his practice of rolling his own cigarettes, and his long handlebar mustache, paired at times, with a goatee. All told, Keogh was "known as the handsomest man in the regiment."[23]

KEOGH WAS AN AMERICAN CITIZEN NOW. FOLLOWING THROUGH ON the feelings he had shared with his brother, Tom, years earlier about the country where he was sure he could get ahead, he was granted his U.S. citizenship on August 25, 1869. Still, his love for Ireland and his family there never wavered, nor his desire to travel back when he could. He hoped and planned for more than the two visits he actually made, but each time he went it meant some six months away from the regiment, a leave of absence that Custer had to okay. More frequent were his trips to Auburn, in upper New York State, to spend time with the Martin family, a much closer respite from cavalry life than a journey across the Atlantic Ocean. His friendship with the Martin daughters, their husbands and boyfriends, grew into the surrogate American family he needed and cherished. Each time he arrived, he was welcomed him as a dear friend, a brother, and a kindly uncle to the children.

Keogh finally made it back to Ireland in August 1869. He was set to go earlier but broke his leg and was laid up, the time recuperating eating into his travel plans. But in an odd turn of events, when he later reinjured the leg, the relapse gave him reason to take a leave of absence and make the trip he had planned earlier. He made his trips via the popular "city" ships of the Inman Line, sailing to Ireland in August 1869 on the City of Paris, and returning to New York the following February on the City of Brooklyn.

In his absence, one wonders who took care of Comanche, giving him the same exacting care as Keogh would have done? Who would have made sure that nothing was passed over in the commander's absence, not the daily grooming or sufficient exercise to keep him as fit as Keogh wanted. While it was never said, it very possibly would have been his close friend, Henry Nowlan, a fellow Irishman, a few years older, who had fought for Britain in the Crimean War.

They had become friends when Nowlan brought his company to reinforce the garrison at Fort Wallace. Keogh had not made close friends with anyone since Kiely and then O'Keefe died, until he and Nowlan developed a close rapport. As horsemen do, they would have spent considerable time with their horses, both riding and at the barn, and Nowlan and Comanche would have come to know each other well. Others may have helped with the hands-on care, but it would be hard to believe that Nowlan didn't keep a watchful eye on Comanche whenever Keogh was away.

It would be nearly five years before Keogh returned to his family, in late May 1874, this time sailing over on the City of Richmond and coming back on the City of Chester. The intervening years had been filled with assignments that made it difficult for him to get away for the time it took for such a visit. As much as he looked forward to going back, it turned out to be a trip that was also a necessity. Keogh, the American cavalry captain, had become lord of historic Castle Clifden in Rathgarvan, a relic from Norman King John, along with the rest of the Blanchfield family estate including some land, and a house in Kilkenny. All had been left to him upon the death of his mother's sister, Aunt Mary Blanchfield, and by Irish law he had only four months to return and claim his inheritance in person. It was a brief tenure as landowner. In keeping with his desire to look out for his family, he ceded all the Blanchfield holdings to his sister, Margaret.

He would return to Ireland soon, he was sure. But he never did. He requested a leave of absence in the spring of 1876, but Custer turned him down. At Fort Abraham Lincoln, Keogh took his place as the most senior captain of the 7th Cavalry, to ride with the regiment from that time forward.

Chapter 7

THE LAST STAND

THE TALK AROUND FORT ABRAHAM LINCOLN THAT SPRING OF 1876 carried a sense of unease. The regiment was to ride out in the coming weeks, heading for the western edge of the Black Hills. It would be a long, difficult trip across territory in which they were unwelcome, the sacred lands of the Lakota Sioux, the largest and most powerful group in the Sioux Nation. Whatever explanations were given to the men of the 7th Cavalry, the suspicion was that there was trouble ahead. The Sioux and their allies in the Northern Plains had not capitulated, many of them still refusing to be forced onto the reservations. If the cavalry thought they could put an end to the difficulties, the Indians had other ideas.

Building blocks that were designed to bring peace to the region—a treaty and the land it protected, and the stated policy of President Ulysses Grant to peacefully assimilate the Plains Indians into the white man's world—all were crumbling. The Second Treaty of Fort Laramie had been signed in 1868, the plan being that by the government giving ownership of the Black Hills to the Lakota Sioux its members would move to the Great Sioux Reservation within the territory. Further, the U.S. agreed that the Indians would be given additional large tracts of hunting lands. The enormous parcel, including the reservation and additional land, extended from the eastern shore of the Missouri River westward to the Bighorn Mountains, south into Nebraska and Colorado, and north into Montana and North Dakota.

To the Lakota Sioux, the Black Hills were sacred. Native peoples had lived on the land for thousands of years, and the histories and myths connected to the vast number of sacred places gave the hills their eternal significance. Moreover, the hills held a precious and albeit very practical resource, an abundance of wild game for times when other food supplies were scarce.

By the terms of the treaty, the land would be off limits to all but the Indians, unless access was granted by them. The treaty was signed by members of a government commission and representatives of various tribes, and began by saying, "From this day forward all war between the parties to this agreement shall forever cease. The Government of the United States desires peace and its honor is hereby pledged to keep it. The Indians desire peace, and they now pledge their honor to maintain it."[1]

Both parties promised retribution if anyone from their side broke the pledge. Many Indians already lived within the reservation area, others moved there. Some lived just outside the reservation but cooperated with the U.S. government and posed no threat. But there were more, however, who would prove a lightning rod, particularly Chief Sitting Bull and his followers, the Hunkpapa Indians. They did not sign the Treaty of Fort Laramie, and they refused to live on the reservation, or abide by any other dictates of the U.S.

A number of forces played into the short life of the treaty that, within a half dozen years, was no longer worth the paper it was written on. Actually, Indian trouble in the region had never really subsided. While Fort Abraham Lincoln was under construction, in 1873-74, it was the target of frequent attacks, as well as raiding parties that made off with mules, horses, and cattle.[2] Trouble escalated by the winter of 1874 to the point that companies were again sent to outpost forts to protect settlers. Keogh, not long back from his trip to Ireland to divest himself of Castle Clifden, led Company I to Fort Totten, about 120 miles northeast of Bismarck on Devil's Lake.

Keogh came into a situation that had started before him. The previous July, while he was still back in Ireland, Custer had led 1,000 men and a mile-long wagon train on a 60-day expedition[3] to explore the Black Hills. The order was to scout possible locations for a fort, but behind that was another reason. It had long been rumored that there was gold in the hills and Custer, with the help of two prospectors he had brought along, was charged with determining if the ore was there and how much there might be.

Custer's report was that there was gold in "paying quantities," information that William E. Curtis, a reporter on the expedition, transmitted in somewhat embellished form to his newspaper, the *Chicago Inter Ocean.*[4] Describing the finds as "pay dirt," the story went on to tell about amounts of gold sufficient to make digging for it worthwhile. Soon it was national news, setting off a second gold rush 26 years after the metal was found at Sutter's Mill in northern California. A double-edged sword, it was welcome news to people in the second year of an economic depression, but very unwelcome news to the Lakota Sioux who, six years before, had been promised absolute rights to the Black Hills. Many Indians still lived off the reservation, and trespassing on their land did not sit well.

Nor was it the first intrusion. Prospectors were already working the land, intent on finding out for themselves if gold was there. But now they flooded in, settlers behind them, and for both groups the Indian troubles grew. The trespassers were in search of wealth, and the sacredness of Indian land was of little concern to them. Moreover, these same intruders demanded protection from the U.S. government, even if they were in a place they should not be.

The government was in a quandary, whether to protect U.S. citizens or uphold a treaty it had signed, and it put Grant's peaceable intensions, his so-called Peace Policy, on the line. But in the end, the choice between whites and Indians wasn't much of a dilemma. The safety of the prospectors and settlers was the priority. The government's initial step, to buy the Black Hills from the Sioux was flatly turned down, its offered price far below what the Indians wanted. The next move was tougher, to make the Indians fall in line by honoring the stipulations of the Treaty of Fort Laramie. The U.S. government would insist that all Indians still living outside the Great Sioux Reservation must move within its borders by the end of 1875. Those who refused would be considered "hostile" and dealt with harshly.

With that, in reality the treaty was essentially null and void. As trespassers onto the Black Hills provoked Indian retaliation, it gave the government license to take a tough stand. On the flip side, Sitting Bull and other Indian leaders who had never signed the Treaty of Fort Laramie dug their heels in deeper. They would not live on the reservation and the word to their tribal members and allies was to do the same. To them, the U.S. government had perpetuated a fraud, the language of peace in the treaty now a hollow promise. The Black Hills, sacred to their world, were also symbolic of the free and nomadic nature of their lives, and to lose the land would threaten their very existence. The Indians did not want to fight. But if they did, they would be fighting for civilization as they knew it.

JANUARY 31, 1876, THE GOVERNMENT'S FINAL DATE BY WHICH Indians must move to the reservation[5] came and went. The holdouts had not cooperated and thus were, in the government's view, open to punitive action. It set in motion an ambitious campaign to force them to capitulate. Cavalry regiments from three forts would head west into present-day southeast Montana, taking the fight to the Indians. The belief was that there were not that many Indians in the area, probably a small encampment that would be fairly easy to overpower. The feeling was the Indians would be startled, even frightened, and readily move to the reservation. It was an inaccurate premise, but it was what guided the military in organizing a campaign that would get underway in the late spring of 1876.

It was a coincidence, but one would imagine frustrating to Keogh that in his ten years with the 7th Cavalry, he had never gone on a campaign with Custer. He served on multiple assignments with the regiment, from Reconstruction duty to accompanying the Northern Boundary Survey. But as well, he needed time to visit his family in Ireland, and deal with the personal difficulties of a broken leg and a relapse from a childhood bout of typhoid fever.

The result was that in the spring of 1876, he had yet to lead his company on one of Custer's expeditions. He had not been part of the regiment's victory in the Battle of the Washita River against a Cheyenne tribe, the Washita Indians in November 1868, nor had he accompanied Custer on the exploration of the Black Hills, frequently considered the opening salvo of what was ahead.

But now Keogh was at Fort Abraham Lincoln, fully present and engaged in helping the 7th Cavalry prepare for their next offensive. Whatever worries he may have had about the future, at this point they were known only to him. His persona, if we are to judge by his Civil War service, was to accept a challenge and exhort his men to follow. Much the same, as they were voicing concerns now meant that Keogh needed to show strength.

Clearly the men were picking up some information, some measure of what was before them. Corporal Thomas Eagan, a member of Company E, was posted to Fort Totten, likely in the winter of 1874 when the cavalry was sent there to combat increased Indian activity in the northeast part of North Dakota. Presumably serving under Keogh, who went there with Company I, Eagan would have been considered one of the captain's boys, as Keogh affectionately called the men in his command. Now in the spring of 1876, talk of the impending expedition had spread to the outpost forts, judging by the letter a worried Eagan wrote to his sister, Ella, in early March.

He would soon be on the move, the destination to be the Bighorn country, he said, adding:

> The Indians are getting bad again. I think that we will have some hard times this summer. The old chief Sitting Bull says he will not make peace with the whites as long as he has a man to fight.

He sent love to family members and told Ella not to write until she heard from him again, then ended, "That is if I do not get my hair lifted by some Indian."[6]

In stark contrast, Keogh's company blacksmith, Henry Allen Bailey, sounded combative and unafraid as he relayed much the same news to his sister, writing from Fort Lincoln, also in early March:

> We expect to go out after Sitting Bull and his cutthroats, and if old Custer gets after him he will give him the fits for all the boys are spoiling for a fight. I only hope they will put it off until about the first of May and then we will not run the risk of freezing to death for its cold weather here now and I had rather be in quarters than out on the prairies in tents.

Bailey closed the letter bragging about his horse, Dan Tucker, who he called, "fat as a pig and feels so good he ran away with me yesterday and ran two miles before I could stop him." He added that he wished his younger brother, Irwin, could visit and ride the horse.[7]

SENDING THE CAVALRY ON THE ROAD WAS NO SMALL FEAT. RATHER, IT was akin to putting the essential (albeit pared down) components of a fort on wheels and on foot. Whether heading out on a trip of exploration, such as the Black Hills Expedition, or to confront the enemy as was the forthcoming plan, preparations got underway months before the projected departure date.

Mounted cavalry each carried over 100 pounds of equipment and ammunition, but it was the multiple mule-hauling wagons that moved the brunt of what was needed to sustain men and horses for as long as they were away from the fort. Food for the men, rations for the horses, bedding, tenting, clothes, ammunition, weapons including Gatling guns, tools, farrier equipment, and more were part of the haul.

Compared to the wagon train that accompanied Keogh and his men from Fort Riley to Fort Wallace ten years before, this one was a huge production. It would leave Fort Abraham Lincoln with 150 vehicles, including six mule wagons each loaded with 5,000 pounds of cargo.[8] All components including cattle for food, and additional horses and mules, filled out a train that stretched for three miles.

Beyond the 30 days of food and horse rations that were packed in the wagons, it was expected that the men would hunt game to augment the usual hardtack-and-bacon diet. Valuable as such interludes were, the hunts were much enjoyed by the men. Not only were buffalo, venison, and other native game a boon to the menus but the horses, lovers of hardtack, likely got more treats. Horses were also allowed to graze as much as possible to fill out their diet, and nature provided fresh water for all. It didn't always work out as well as might be hoped, but that was the plan.

As one of the four new cavalries organized after the close of the Civil War, the 7th Cavalry benefitted from a step up in veterinary care. Lincoln's disgust at the condition of horses in that war had moved him to initiate some important changes at the regimental level. They started post war with the addition of two staff members, senior and junior veterinary surgeons, whose singular focus was the condition of the horses.

Not surprisingly, filling the posts and keeping them thus, if the situation at the 7th Cavalry was a typical example, was not easy. The first to accept the post of senior veterinary surgeon, Dr. John Honsinger, was killed in a Sioux ambush in 1873, less than a year after accepting the position. It was a sad blow as the doctor had served through the Civil War with distinction, and was known as an exceptionally fine and dedicated horseman who loved the animals for their own sake.[9]

After Honsinger, other doctors came and left in quick succession until Dr. Charles A. Stein arrived from New Orleans in April 1876, accompanied by a herd of mules,[10] all in time for the spring campaign. Stein's first concern was to inspect all the cavalry horses to determine their fitness for the expedition ahead. More specifically, he needed to determine which horses were unserviceable and which others, with some further conditioning, would be in good shape for coming demands.

Nothing specific has been said about Comanche, but under Keogh's doting care it would be a good guess that the reliable mustang was fit and ready for action. According to one observer, "He could work harder and keep in good flesh on less feed than any other horse in the regiment." Neither hot or cold weather seemed to make any difference to him, the admirer continued, "He had an easy, fast gait; could carry a man on a hard, all-day march and be fresh all the time."[11]

THE CAMPAIGN TO BRING DOWN THE LAKOTAS AND OTHERS OF THE Sioux Nation, along with their allies, the Northern Cheyenne and the Arapaho, would be complicated but based on its sweeping design was expected to achieve success with relative ease.

General Philip Sheridan, post-Civil War head of the Division of the Missouri, that covered the enormous stretch of the American Plains from the Mississippi River to the Rocky Mountains, had designated three cavalry forces from three separate forts to converge in the area of the Little Bighorn Valley of Montana. Riding under his command would be General Alfred Terry, commander of the Department of the Dakotas and Custer's commander.

Terry, Custer, and the 12 companies of the 7th regiment, plus a couple hundred infantry also based at the fort, would head west from Fort Abraham Lincoln. Major General John Gibbon, commander of the U.S. 7th Infantry, would bring his column of 450 men east from Fort Ellis near Bozeman, Montana, and Major General George Crook would lead 1,000 men, a mix of cavalry and infantry, north from Fort Fetterman in Wyoming Territory.

The troops would meet near the Little Bighorn River, where it was expected that Indians were about to celebrate the spring solstice with their annual Sun Dance, a ceremony of spiritual and creative renewal after the long winter. The encampment, if it followed previous years, would be of moderate size, perhaps 2,000 Indians of which 800 or so would be fighting men, specifically warriors and teenage boys. However the plan was worked out, the commanders Sheridan had chosen and their men should be able to handle whatever they encountered. At Fort Lincoln, the departure date was set for May 17, 1876.

This would be the first time since its establishment that the entire 7th Cavalry, all 12 companies of the regiment, would fight together. Was it the size and scope of the operation, a realization that the manpower being sent out by Terry and Custer was only a part of what was heading toward the Little Bighorn, and what was at stake there that clouded Keogh's thoughts? Despite his brave face, even he had grown concerned, enough to let down his guard in a letter to Nelly Martin back in Auburn, New York:

> We leave Monday on an Indian expedition & if I ever return I will go on and see you all. I have requested to be packed up and shipped to Auburn in case I am killed, and I desire to be buried there. God bless you all, remember if I should die - you may believe that I loved you and every member of your family - it was a second home to me.[12]

This one time, Keogh let his emotions give us a glimpse, perhaps, into the depth of the relationship between him and Nelly. He didn't write his family that we know of, possibly not to worry them, but he did write to her.

His other step could be viewed as more the practical measure of an active-duty soldier. He had chased enough Indians in his time at Fort Wallace and Fort Totten to remember how unpredictable combat with them could be. Thus, he asked Mrs. Eliza Porter, the wife of his Company I assistant, Lieutenant James Porter, to burn a satchel of his personal papers should he be killed. He already had life insurance, the $10,000 policy he had purchased three years ago in Minnesota, while he was waiting at Fort Snelling for the Northern Boundary Survey to get underway. The men with him then, who had followed his lead, were likely feeling comforted by that now.

Leave taking on May 17 was later than Terry would have liked, delayed by the remnants of a winter that had been long and harsh in that part of the country. Keogh had thought it would be Monday, but it wasn't until Wednesday when everything was in readiness, the men, their horses, and the enormous pack train to support them from Fort Lincoln and back. Any time the regiment saddled up and marched out the front gates, the Stars and Stripes and company flags held high as they proceeded, was a festive occasion. But this day Terry asked for even more pomp and ceremony to reassure the families of the departing men that the cavalry would triumph over adversity.[13] Mount up was the clarion call.

KEOGH WAS AT THE STALL BEFORE DAWN, PERHAPS A LITTLE EARLIER than usual, to make sure that Comanche had a good breakfast and plenty of time to eat his hay. Both could feel the crackle in the air, the horse knowing as well as his owner that today would be different. Likely Keogh gave him a little more brushing that morning, just to bring out the gold glints in Comanche's coat.

The two had ridden together for eight years, a long time in the rough and dangerous world of the cavalry, and they had acquitted themselves well on assignments in the South, at the Northern border, and on the Plains. But this day they would embark on the most challenging undertaking of their military careers, a long, taxing campaign that would ask for the best from both horse and rider.

They understood each other, as good partners do. Comanche had come to know what Keogh expected, a willingness to go the extra measure, to be brave when he must. Keogh had trained Comanche to perfection, and the horse had trained his owner, too. Keogh would have known how Comanche liked to be brushed and rubbed down, the treats he preferred, and what men of the regiment had his approval. Keogh's best friend, Nowlan, would show himself to be one of them.

They made an impressive pair, the proud Irish-American cavalryman and his tough, quintessentially American Mustang. With Comanche tacked up, Keogh, the regiment's most senior captain, hoisted himself into the saddle and they took their place alongside Custer and Victory. Two by two, the members of the 7th Cavalry fell in behind them, the line of men on their horses stretching back as it wound its way across the fort grounds.

The regimental band was playing *The Girl I Left Behind,* an 18th century Irish folk song that had been a favorite of both sides in the Civil War. You could hear the men singing, a melodic droning, words coming through here and there as they trotted by. Then smoothly they swung into the 7th's marching song, *Garryowen,* with that picking up an easy canter as they rode through the fort's main gate.

It was mostly a sea of blue, riders in dark blue cavalry blouses (as shirts were called then) and trousers, hats with medium-wide brims and high crowns, and bandanas. The latter were usually yellow, although Custer was known for wearing bandanas of red silk. Colorful accessories they were, but even more handy for covering nose and mouth when caught in a bug storm or billowing dust. In the field, there was a much greater variety of clothing and headgear, cavalry blues and light-colored buckskins worn as both blouses and trousers, brimmed hats or campaign caps, and always spurs.

If there had been worry knots in some stomachs, they were ignored on this day by the proud cavalrymen and their quick-stepping horses. They were, after all, the renown 7th Cavalry and glad to be. Just like Sergeant Charles Windolph said of that send-off to the Little Bighorn:

> You felt like you were somebody when you were on a good horse, with a carbine dangling from its small leather ring socket on your McClellan saddle, and a Colt army revolver strapped on your hip; and a hundred rounds of ammunition in your web belt and in your saddle pockets. You were a cavalryman of the Seventh Regiment. You were a part of a proud outfit that had a fighting reputation, and you were ready for a fight or a frolic.[14]

But even as wives and children, girlfriends and all the others staying behind waved and cheered in the tradition of giving their men a rousing send-off, there were tears and worry on some faces. Libbie Custer later admitted that she had dreamt of bodies falling from the sky.[15] Curiously, Sitting Bull told his followers of a similar vision, of many dead soldiers "falling right into our camp."[16] To him it meant his people would win a great victory.

THE THREE COLUMNS WERE TO MEET UP AT THE EDGE OF THE LITTLE Bighorn Valley on June 26, six weeks from then. It was not planned that they would unite as a coordinated strike force, but rather that they could provide enough fire power to deal with whatever they found, be it a single village or bands of roving Indians moving on.[17] In that great spread of country, with men coming from three far-flung locations, there would be no further communication, only expectations for when they met.

Neither Terry or Custer knew until much later that Crook didn't show up because his men had been caught in a surprise attack by a large band of Sioux and Cheyenne near Rosebud Creek east of the Bighorn River. He was close to the agreed upon destination, but his force sustained a number of deaths and injuries, and Crook was forced to withdraw from the march and regroup. Nor did the men of the 7th know why Gibbon's infantry weren't ready to fight when anticipated, because his infantry took two days longer than planned to make the trip from western Montana. All the men of the 7th knew was that they were the only ones positioned to press on and, apparently, they were on their own.

Working their way across the Dakota Territory—in 1876 still 13 years away from becoming North and South Dakota—the cavalry moved west-south-west into the southeastern corner of Montana, setting up a base camp on the Powder River June 10. It was the stopping point for the big wagons, Custer's hunting dogs that often accompanied him when he rode out, and the band.

Grateful to be left to guard the depot were sixty-odd late recruits to the 7th Cavalry, forced to walk the distance from Fort Lincoln as there were not enough horses for them. It is thought that Stein, the veterinary surgeon, was detached at that point, as well.[18] Pressing on from there were cavalrymen, their officers, Indian scouts, the two-horse pack trains with reduced provisions, and extra horses. The band struck up *Garryowen* one more time, the strains fading as the cavalry moved into the distance.

TWO WEEKS HENCE THEY WOULD FACE AN INDIAN FIGHTING FORCE three times what they expected. The many camps stretched side by side along the edge of the Little Bighorn River for three miles, in all perhaps 1,000 lodges belonging to the member tribes of the Sioux Nation—the Hunkpapa, Oglala, Miniconjou, Sans Arc, Blackfoot, and Northern Cheyenne— and other Indians that would fight with them.

The Indians called their river the Greasy Grass because of how the swaying plants on the bottom appeared through the clear water. It was well known that tribes made their way to the area every spring. But this year's numbers were far greater than usual, the Indians answering Sitting Bull's call for a showing of strength against the U.S. government. It had branded them "hostile" because they would not live on the reservation, to the Indians a sign that their tribal ways were marked for elimination.

Numbers vary widely, but conservatively it is thought there were at least 8,000 Indians of all ages, 2,000 to 2,500 of them warriors ready to fight. Unfortunately, if anyone knew the reality of the situation, it wasn't transmitted to commanders in the field, at least certainly not in time.

The cavalry pushed on, from the depot on the Powder River continuing to follow river after river, the Yellowstone to the Bighorn and, finally, the Little Bighorn. The pace overall averaged a moderate 16 (or thereabouts) miles a day. Some days they pushed hard and long, other days they slacked off giving the men a rest and the horses more grazing time.

Unfortunately, for the horses it didn't work as well as planned. The caravan carried half rations for the horses, expecting that good spring grazing would more than make up the difference. But the grasslands were poor and worse, some of the freshwater streams were alkaline and bitter-tasting from the winter run-off. Comanche, the tough Mustang, dealt with the lacking nutrition with his usual equanimity, but other horses weren't as resilient.

On most of these long expeditions, there were horses that gave out entirely, but on this march the walking pace apparently saved a number from that pitiful end.

THE PACKET BOAT *FAR WEST* BROUGHT AN ADDED LOAD OF SUPPLIES from Fort Lincoln, sailing down the Missouri, the Yellowstone, and the Bighorn rivers and tying up at the mouth of the Little Bighorn, at that point the water too shallow to proceed farther. Three days from the anticipated confrontation, a select group went onboard for an evening of drinking and playing cards, among them Keogh, Custer, Grant Marsh, the captain of the *Far West*. Also on board was a Lieutenant Garland, a lawyer in civilian life, who Keogh asked to draw up his will. He gave it to Nowlan, by then the 7th Cavalry's Regimental Quartermaster, with instructions to send it to Keogh's sister if he didn't return. Though the sister was unnamed, we can guess it was Margaret, by then with a castle and land to maintain.[19]

The evening on the *Far West* marked the divide between the preamble and the main event, of almost six weeks of travel capped by a fast-moving end game. The column from Fort Abraham Lincoln was now at the entrance to the Little Bighorn Valley, a broad plain formed of ridges cut by ravines and coulees or small streams. The geography worked for both sides, the ridges providing good views across the valley and defensible heights for the cavalry. The ravines and coulees offered hiding places for the Indians, who then attacked from them. The meandering, north flowing Little Bighorn River, a tributary of the Bighorn River, was shallow enough so as not to hinder either side, whether attacking or retreating.

On June 22, Terry changed his plans, splitting the Fort Lincoln column and directing Custer to take the entire 7th regiment south in a wide swing that generally followed Rosebud Creek, then cut across to the Little Bighorn below the expected location of the Indian camp. Terry would stay north, approaching the camp from that end in a combined effort to be executed on June 26. But Custer heard what he wanted.

Historians often refer to him as the boy general for his exemplary service during the Civil War, his increased responsibility rewarded with higher ranks as the conflict continued. Post war, his command of the 7th Cavalry was equally applauded. His victory over the Washitas eight years before resulted from a surprise attack at dawn that awakened the tribe, killing many unsuspecting members but causing few casualties among the cavalry. Five years later, he also assisted the government's position to take back the Black Hills with his expedition into that region.

But along with his successes, Custer also incurred Grant's fury when he implicated the president's brother in a federal corruption case. Grant retaliated by barring the general from participation in the Little Bighorn campaign, and only through the intercession of other commanders did the president reverse his position. It is thought that Custer saw his involvement, indeed a victory in whatever battle lay ahead, as the chance to get back in Grant's good graces. If Custer had political ambitions, as he may have, Grant's support would have been important.

The Battle of the Little Bighorn, Custer believed, could follow the same pattern as the Battle of the Washitas, a sunrise attack on June 26. The difference was that the Washita's camp was small and this, unbeknownst until very late in the game, was big. What is puzzling is that when Custer sent out scouts to find the camp, the information they brought back, that it was far bigger than anyone expected, he didn't accept. Was he so vested in the script he had written that he could not bring himself to adjust to what was actually unfolding? We know only that his refusal to yield to what his scouts told him came too late, and he and his men rode into a totally untenable situation.

Trouble in the early hours of June 25 altered the first change in the battle as Custer had planned it. Keogh and his Company I had pulled mule duty which, at this point, entailed getting the mules with their cargo strapped to their backs across a muddy, boggy stretch of water. It was a maddening detail, the mules braying as they struggled against the footing, the pack ropes loosening, and Keogh's temper flaring. Getting nowhere fast, the problem boxes were cut loose and left at the water's edge for someone to retrieve early in the morning.[20]

Though the story from there varies depending on the historian, the result was the same. The cargo was not retrieved in time, forfeiting the element of surprise. Whether the boxes were taken before one of Keogh's men showed up, presumably carried off by Indians or, per another story, the soldier came upon an Indian about to take the boxes and shot him, the Lakota Sioux was quickly alerted that the cavalry was close at hand.[21]

With the hope to surprise the enemy gone, Custer made the choice that would seal their fate. Against Terry's order to wait until June 26, Custer chose the time-honored commander's approach and forged ahead. He divided the 12 companies into four battalions: one company would remain in the rear with the pack train; three companies under Captain Frederick Benteen, a total of 125 men, would stay south, looking for additional Indian locations, and ready to support the other companies when needed; three companies under Major Marcus Reno, in all 140 men, would attack the camp at its south end; and the remaining five companies, 210 men under Custer, would move upstream to attack the heart of the village. Of those five companies, he turned two or three over to Keogh's command, Company I, which had been his all along, Company F and Company L. Unknown still was how many Indians they would face.

Once troops were assembled Keogh made his own significant change. Comanche was brought up from the pack and held while Keogh shifted the tack from Paddy, settled his McClellan saddle on Comanche's back, tightened the girth, and swung into the saddle. Comanche had walked with the herd from Fort Lincoln, cared for by Keogh just as he did Paddy. But now Paddy's job was done and it was his turn to head to the rear. He had carried the captain safely to this point. Comanche would handle the rest.

Custer, Keogh, and Reno, at the head of their assembled companies began moving north along a ridge, following the Little Bighorn somewhere south of the Indian camp. From their elevation they began to see lodges across the river on the west bank, signaling the time for Reno to make his move. He would cross the Little Bighorn and attack at the camp's south end, hoping he could surprise the Indians who would then scatter and be killed.

Custer and Keogh, their men following, turned back and retook the ridge. It was the last time that anyone saw them alive. Reno, heading north on the other side of the river, charged into the first of the afternoon's debacles. The Indians were ready for him and upended his planned offensive, turning it into a merciless and bloody retreat to high ground. The companies suffered many dead and wounded, but still continued to fend off the harassment of Indians into the next day.

FROM THE MOMENT CUSTER AND KEOGH DISAPPEARED FROM VIEW, save a couple more glimpses as they moved in and out of tree cover along the ridge, the rest of what happened that afternoon of June 25, 1876 at The Last Stand, was known only to those who survived what came to be known as the worst battle of the American Indian wars. Archaeological explorations and the considered opinions of historians and others have filled the void with much that is probable, but not more. The eyes-on accounts came from the Indians who were there. The 210 men who fought, including Custer and Keogh, perished.

But deductions can be made, first that the men proceeded along the river until more and more of the camp came into view, and with it appeared movement among the Indians that made it clear they were ready for a fight. A scrawled note by Custer's adjutant, Lieutenant William Cooke, was carried at a gallop to Benteen by trumpeter John Martin, for him a life-saving mission. The terse message said: Come on. Big village. Be quick. Bring packs. P.S. Bring packs.[22]

Custer was calling for more ammunition. But Benteen didn't respond, having come upon Reno's badly beaten and retreating contingent still being hammered by Indians. At Reno's urging, Benteen stayed to help him. If he had gone to help Custer, would it have made a difference? Almost a century and a half later, historians are still debating.

Upstream, having forded the river and carried the attack to the Indians, Custer and Keogh were met with almost unfathomable odds, some say as high as 20 to one. Indian deaths were met with fierce reprisals, the waves of fighting interspersed with Indians taking the dead men's clothing and rifles, and their frantic, runaway horses. Custer pushed to attain a high position, ultimately what is today known as Last Stand Hill. Keogh, enabling Custer's moves, held his company to skirmish lines downhill from where Custer fought.

Time and events raced by, likely less than an hour from when Custer first engaged his enemy until all was quiet. One Indian said it lasted about "as long as it took to eat a meal."[23] At the end, the Indians threw a virtual noose around Custer's position, tightened by Chief Crazy Horse and his Oglalas coming from the North and Chief Gall and his Hunkpapas from the south.[24] Finally, within the diminished circle, all men and horses died, a fitting coup for Gall whose two wives and three children were among the first killed by Custer.[25]

Keogh kept his skirmish lines solid as long as he could, until at the last he and his men were overrun. Indians said he stayed on Comanche the whole time, exhorting his dismounted men to hold fast, at one point actually turning his horse broadside to shield his troops. In death, he lay amidst a number of the men of Company I, including two lieutenants, the standard bearer, and the trumpeter, testament perhaps to the regard in which they held their commander.

He was known as a brave, aggressive fighter, and the Indians recalled nothing less in his final moments. At the end, the Gall warrior, Little Soldier, told of Keogh astride Comanche as a bullet entered the horse's chest on a diagonal, exiting at his rider's left knee and shattering it. The Indian identified Keogh as a "bluecoat" and said, thrown from the horse, he dragged himself under Comanche and continued firing from between his front legs, glaring wildly as if he was from the spirit world. A warrior shot him in the head, Keogh dying with Comanche's reins still gripped in one hand. Little Soldier needed a horse and would have taken Comanche, but not when the reins were held by a dead man.[27] The Indians also believed that it was bad luck to take a horse that was so closely attuned to its owner, even one who had died.[28] Comanche was steadfast to the very end, and that bond protected them both, the Indians leaving them as they were.

RENO'S MEN HAD ESCAPED TO A HILL ABOUT FOUR MILES SOUTH FROM where Custer was fighting. The air must have been still because in the late afternoon sounds were carrying, heavy bursts of gunfire interspersed with stillness. After what turned out to be the last round of fire, some of Reno's officers headed north. About a mile and a half up, they looked out from a promontory to see, in the distance, plumbs of smoke and dust rising and within the area Indians jumping and firing at the ground.

One of the officers, Captain Thomas Weir, said he didn't think they were fighting but, instead, killing the wounded, as was the Indian custom of "putting an extra bullet or arrow into an enemy's body [as] a gesture of triumph."[26] If the men had still intended to proceed, they were blocked by Indians who forced them back to Reno's position.

It wouldn't have mattered. The Last Stand was over.

Chapter 8

ENDING AND BEGINNING

THE STENCH HUNG IN THE HOT AIR, HARSH YET FAMILIAR, THE LIGHT breeze moving it slowly toward them across the rolling hills. It was a warning they didn't need. They knew, even as they didn't want to acknowledge it, what was coming. The severe winter had given way to a broiling summer. After being scorched by the sun for two days, the men's bodies were blackened and bloated, the horses' bodies only bloated. The scene was horrific, terrifying to look at but difficult to turn away from.

Terry and Gibbon had received the news the day before, June 26, as they and several hundred troops were making their way southward, beyond the mouth of the Little Bighorn River, expecting to connect with Custer and his forces. As planned, it was to be the start of the operation but, instead, they met three of Custer's Crow Indian scouts coming back up the valley. In sign language, they told the commanders that all the white men had been killed the day before.[1] Not fully accepting what they heard, Terry and Gibbon pushed on and soon connected with Reno's battered contingent, at that point understanding more of what happened. It still wasn't the whole story, but seeing what had befallen Reno and his men, a worst-case scenario was crowding out other possibilities.

The next morning, June 27, Terry sent Benteen and some of his men to find Custer and piece together the rest of the story. A trip that two days ago would have seemed completely unnecessary or, at worst, a rescue party, now would be a burial detail after a battle that wiped out five companies of the U.S. 7th Cavalry. Riding up to the battlefield, about four miles from where they left Reno's detachment, they could see bodies of men and horses everywhere, their dying places a picture of how the battle played out. Bodies lay across each other, falling as their skirmish lines had collapsed and been overrun; others were in ravines, at the water's edge, or floating in the river, as they attempted to flee; 30 to 40 others were with Custer on what, in time, would be called Last Stand Hill. It was the highest point of the battlefield, and Custer and some of his men and officers had hoped from there they could fight back against the encroaching Indians. Instead, in a scene that suggested fast-approaching doom, Indians rushed them from all sides, closing off any chance of escape until the men had no way out.

Walking their horses carefully among the dead, some riders dismounting and leading them, Benteen's men made a swift count: 210 men, officers and soldiers, lay dead; also according to their count, 70 cavalry horses and two Indian ponies.[2] The Indians had already taken their dead away. The number of them killed was never adequately established and still, today, ranges from 30 to 300.[3] Soon after the battle, the Indians admitted to a higher number of deaths, but in later pictographs it was corrected downward.

Some of the horses, pitifully, were not quite dead, but the men took care of that as quickly as they could, ending each one's misery with a clean shot to the head. A sense of the booty taken by the Indians was clear in the many more horses that had not died with their riders. Considering the 225 that had delivered troops to the battle[4] (one for each cavalryman plus extras), some 150 had been run off, a common occurrence when fighting the Indians.

Certainly, many never made it past a battle, killed by the Indians, or by the cavalrymen themselves to use in a downed position as their last, desperate shield against enemy bullets. But when the Indians were victors, any potentially useful horses, even injured ones that could be healed, were not left. They were stampeded by Indian women who came on the field during lulls in the fighting or at the end, waving buffalo rugs at the horses after their riders had been shot off, or after they panicked and tore loose while being held behind a skirmish line. In that case, four riders had dismounted, one falling back and holding four horses while the other three men would stand (or kneel) and fire at the enemy in a skirmish line. In the years of Indian conflict, when cavalrymen or government representatives had reason to be in an Indian village, often they saw these survivors, horses with "US" branded on their flank that had been taken in battle.

HORSES WERE THE INDIANS' LIFEBLOOD AND THEY TOOK ANY THEY could use, but whether they survived was another matter. Indian horses lived on the plains near a village, turned out all year long to eat prairie grasses and, in the winter, forage for what they could find. Abruptly, with no time to transition from the diet they knew, the stolen cavalry horses were forced to do the same. Some adapted, but others used to the white man's diet of grain and hay, wasted away and died.

There was one horse who would have managed well, reverting to his first years living off the Texas desert. He had been coveted by an Indian, too, but the assumed mystical connection to his rider had scared the admirer away. Even left where he was, his toughness kept him alive, and then saved his life. Two days later, he was still on the battlefield, wounded, bloodied and beaten-looking, the saddle swung under his belly and hanging by the girth so the weight pulled on his back. Descriptions varied as to exactly what position he was in, whether standing on all fours or settled back on his haunches, and whether he was in a ravine trying to get to water or somewhere else on the field.

No matter how he looked, seeing him was the one glad moment that morning. Comanche, Captain Keogh's horse, had survived, and upon hearing the men talking, had whinnied his presence. Likely, it was Nowlan's voice, so familiar to Comanche, that stood out above the rest and that he answered.[5] Nowlan and others went right to him, bringing him water, grass to eat, washing his wounds and cleaning the dried blood that was caked to his coat. By then more comfortable, he was given what he reportedly liked best, a bran mash liberally wetted down with Hennessey. Possibly emptying the whole bottle,[6] it was certainly a caring gift for the owner to part with his fine brandy. Over time, a number of the men seemed to remember being the first to recognize Comanche, surely a praiseworthy thing to have done. Nowlan never said otherwise; he just made sure that from then on his friend's horse was well cared for. Keogh was gone and, in a sense, Comanche now belonged to the regiment. And he was coming home with them.

THE TERRIBLE TASK AT HAND WAS TO BURY 210 OF THEIR FELLOW soldiers. In one way or another, all but two had been mutilated. Many were horribly disfigured, the details of what had been done to their bodies beyond what anyone ever wanted to see or remember. To the Indians it was an act of revenge, as such a part of their code of justice. They believed by defacing their victims, they were forced to go to the afterlife in that terrible state.[7] It was retribution for a war they did not want, and not only did victims go to the next life altered, but the pain also slowed their journey. Years later, as Indians told their stories, they dodged talk of what they had done to their victims, some admitting to the horror but disavowing any knowledge of who did it.[8]

Details of what happened to the men were known within the military, but it was many years before outside sources tapped into the information and relayed it to the public more graphically. Perhaps with reverence for the deceased and their families, and reflecting what would be considered appropriate descriptions then, Lieutenant Bradley, one of Terry's officers, sent a carefully worded version of what befell the men to the *Helena Weekly* in Montana, on July 27, a month after the battle:

> Of the 206 bodies buried on the field, there were very few that I did not see, and beyond scalping, in possibly a majority of cases, there was little mutilation. Many of the bodies were not even scalped, and in the comparatively few cases of disfiguration it appeared to me rather the result of a blow than of a knife.[9]

The death count, in that period and later, varied by sources. It is also thought some bodies were missed by the first burial detail as, in later years, unidentified human bones turned up on the battlefield.

THE DEAD WERE STRIPPED OF THEIR CLOTHING, THEIR POCKETS ransacked for valuables. Keogh among them had been left naked except for his socks but, otherwise, the Indians did nothing to mar his body. The reasons for their tempered treatment of the captain have puzzled historians since, but any of three possibilities seem likely. For one, he always wore a Papal medal in a leather pouch around his neck, though whether it was the *Pro Petri Sede* or the *Order of St. Gregory*, we don't know. The Indians might have seen it as a powerful talisman, similar to the ones that they carried,[10] and as it glinted in the sun, it might have warned them not to touch Keogh further.

They say, too, that as he died he kept hold of Comanche's reins, a connection that even as it loosened and they took his clothes, the Indians saw as a more powerful force than anything they wanted to disturb. Or lastly, and perhaps most profoundly, as Chief Red Horse said later, on behalf of many Sioux, "... this man was the bravest man they had ever met"[11] and that reason alone may have meant the difference between mutilating him and leaving him alone.

Yet, whether as a token of a brave man, or just because the items were there for the taking, the Indians stole Keogh's gauntlets with his name on them, and the Company I guidon, the men's battle flag. The items were recovered, the gauntlets wrapped in the guidon, on September 9, 1876 in the tipi of Chief American Horse, after he was killed and his village burned.[12] As to other Keogh memorabilia, his custom-made English revolver was later discovered in Canada, but the Indian who had it wouldn't sell. As to the medal around his neck, some contend that photographs of Sitting Bull years later showed him wearing it the same way.

The other soldier who was spared from being mutilated was Custer, and that was certainly true in relation to what was done to his men. But it was not entirely the case. He was shot twice, both bullets deemed fatal, but decades later a story emerged that added an interesting layer to his final state. As the narrative goes, two Indian women came onto the battlefield after the fighting was over and found Custer's body. They shooed away a warrior who was about to deface him, saying they were his relatives. They had with them large buffalo bone needles, the type used to repair tipis. But now they plunged them into his ear drums, telling him it would help him to hear better in the afterlife, and never again to break promises. They reminded him of two promises he made, one to an Indian maiden and the niece of one of the women. They said she had an affair with Custer eight years before, bearing him two children before he left her, not caring that in Cheyenne culture he and the young woman were married. She loved him still, they said, and wept for him. Nor did he hear his promise never to fight the Indians, and that, the women said, would also not happen in the afterlife.[13] But to the men who buried him, the stab wounds went unnoticed, and Custer like Keogh was considered unscathed.

Over two days, the dead were buried as quickly as could be done, in shallow graves marked with the men's names on slips of paper, caught by a slit in the end of a stick and stuck into the ground. The graves were planned as temporary sites, permanent burials to be the following year, when the wishes of the families to have their loved ones remain on the battleground or be reinterred elsewhere would be carried out. Custer would be buried at West Point and Keogh would return to his second home in Auburn, New York.

Temporary turned out to be more than a descriptive word for the gravesites, as Army personnel found out when they returned in 1877. The Custer grave, with George and his brother, Tom, originally buried together, had been torn apart and the skeletons spread about, presumably by coyotes.[14] It was never said otherwise, but that the animals stopped their rampage with only one grave would have been hard to believe. Those bodies who were never claimed, were also reinterred on the battlefield, in a cemetery established near Last Stand Hill. The horses were left where they had fallen for nature to take its course, as it did. The resulting pile of sun-bleached bones were buried together in a specially created horse grave. A white grave marker honors all of them, too, the horses who also served.

ON JUNE 28, BENTEEN AND THE BURIAL CONTINGENT MADE THEIR WAY the four miles back to where Reno and the remaining men waited. Comanche, cared for indulgently and gaining strength, made the walk without difficulty, nothing to the contrary ever reported. The survivors of Reno's command had moved down from the bluff to the valley floor, there the injured further treated while preparations were made to move everyone out of the area. The battalion had been decimated, sustaining 32 dead and 54 wounded in two days of fighting.[15] Not only had the Indians come after Reno's troops when they retreated from the Indian village on June 25, but they chased them to the bluff (later called Reno Hill), continuing to attack through the night and into the next day. One surgeon had died with Custer, leaving only Dr. Porter to cope with the aftermath.

Twenty miles up the valley, the *Far West* was still moored at the mouth of the Little Bighorn River. In the previous week, Terry had used the ship as his headquarters, but since his departure, Captain Marsh and his crew had waited for what they hoped would be good news, but with nagging concern. Custer's Crow scout, Curly, had happened upon the ship earlier, telling a barely intelligible story of terrible fighting.[16] It was garbled and confused, a mix of signing, words, and pictures, and they hoped somehow the story was wrong. But shortly, they would be stunned to learn that Curly spoke the truth —followed by a demand of the *Far* West that would challenge Marsh and his crew.

Starting out late on June 28, they traveled well into the night to escape the heat and mosquitoes. Terry, Gibbon, and the combined Reno-Benteen command were starting a difficult trek, men walking, hobbling, and the most seriously wounded carried on litters. It was a frustratingly slow pace, the column managing only four and a half miles north before making camp opposite where Custer and his men were now buried. The Indians had left their camps and disappeared but, amongst the refuse, discarded tipi poles suggested a way to increase the pace. The poles would be strapped to mules, one on either side, and the litters lashed between them, with the trailing ends of the poles held up by the men.

The mule litters sped things up enough that, rather than break the trip one more time, they pushed on the rest of the way the next night, June 29. Terry rode ahead to tell Marsh of the disaster that had been, and what was needed now. By the time the column arrived, Marsh and his men had spread grass all over the deck and covered it with blankets. The wounded were onboard and bedded down by 2:00 a.m., July 30, the able bodied still ashore, to continue the trip overland. There was sorrow among them for their dead colleagues, but a profound sense of gratitude to have survived a brutal battle.

No one was more adept at sailing the Missouri River and its tributaries in those years than Captain Grant Marsh. His great skill as a river pilot, capable of maneuvering in waters shallower than anyone else would attempt, is what brought the *Far West* down the Bighorn River all the way to the mouth of the Little Bighorn. Called a packet boat or steamboat, the advantage she had, that Marsh used so well, was that the *Far West* drew only 20 inches. Though that was when unloaded, it meant that even with cargo it could make it through the shallow Bighorn, since the hull didn't reach far below the waterline. Plus, as a sternwheeler, with one paddle wheel aft, it could navigate through narrower rivers than the other popular steamboat model, the side-wheeler. It was for those reasons that the U.S. Army wanted Marsh and his ship in its service for the campaign of 1876.

The captain was in his 40s then, already a veteran of many years sailing on the Missouri, beginning as a cabin boy and working his way up to his first captaincy ten years before his encounter with the Little Bighorn. The Missouri River could be treacherous, with rushing currents, wide swings in her flow, and shifting channels, sandbars, underwater timbers, and more. Yet, through Marsh's skill, the *Far West* sailed the Missouri system for 13 years, well beyond the usual lifespan for steamboats that, on average, was five years before they cracked up from one of the river's dangers.

The ship had a reputation for speed, but never more than it showed that summer. With the wounded settled and secure, Marsh headed back into the Bighorn River and north to the Yellowstone River, there to spend two days ferrying Gibbon's troops across its expanse. Leaving there on July 3, with Marsh and his co-pilot, Dave Campbell, spelling each other every four hours around the clock,[17] they traveled down the Missouri to deliver their passengers to Fort

Abraham Lincoln in record time. The trip of more than 700 miles in 54 hours by a steamboat was never equaled or broken.[18] One of the wounded men died during the trip and they made a stop at the Powder River Depot to bring his body ashore. Then, as they neared their destination, the crew draped the ship's exterior in black crepe paper and lowered the flag to half mast, and at 11:00 p.m. on July 5, 1876, Marsh docked the *Far West* at Fort Lincoln.

With that, the news was out. The families waiting at Fort Lincoln, especially the women and children keeping vigil for their men, were overwhelmed with shock and grief seeing the ship in its funereal dressing. Whatever their worries, the frightening images and nightmares, they had been suppressed by hope for the safe return of their husbands, brothers, fathers, and lovers, who they had seen off less than two months before. It is said that Marsh accompanied one of the officers, going home to home to bring the news to each family individually. As shaken as she was, Libbie Custer pulled herself together and went with them, believing that as the commander's wife she should be there, too. Nine years later, speaking for herself and the many others, she wrote in her memoir, *Boots and Saddles* (1885): "This battle wrecked the lives of 26 women at Fort Lincoln, and orphaned children of officers and soldiers joined their cry to that of their bereaved mothers."[19]

AS SOON AS THE NEWS WAS DELIVERED TO HIM, THE TELEGRAPH operator at Bismarck began transmitting the story, and newspapers from coast to coast ran their first reports on June 6. The *Bismarck Tribune* put out an "Extra" with the story, as did the *San Diego Union*, while the *New York Times* published a lengthy story that told the history of the Little Bighorn campaign from its start. Other newspapers added their reports over the next days and weeks, including accounts from the Indians' point of view.

But it was two Montana newspapers that scooped the others,

breaking their stories of the disastrous battle on June 3 and 4. Their reports were based on a dispatch written by Terry on June 27, to be delivered by courier to the commanding officer of Fort Ellis, Captain D.W. Benham of the 7th Infantry, with further instructions to have the telegraph office at Bozeman send it out nationally. The *Bozeman Times* released the story as an "Extra" edition the evening of June 3.[20]

Because of one lucky break, however, it was the *Helena Herald*, that stole the spotlight. Problems with transmission limited how far Bozeman could send their story, but enroute to Fort Ellis, the courier had met a correspondent for the Helena newspaper and told him the news he had. The reporter went directly to his paper, and the *Herald* broke the story as an "Extra" on July 4, during the city's Fourth of July celebration. Then, instead of Bozeman's telegraph, it was the *Herald* that sent the story to the Associated Press at Salt Lake City, from where it went to papers countrywide, some of them pushing the story out in late editions on June 5, and more on June 6.[21] The country was collectively horrified, outraged, sobered, bewildered. People demanded explanations, answers, retribution. Fingers were pointed every which way. President Grant called the debacle a "sacrifice of troops" by Custer, while others vilified Reno and Benteen.[22] Within a few years, a formal court of inquiry was held.

By the time Comanche came back to Fort Lincoln, the initial excitement for the men who made it home had died down, and his return home was without fanfare. It wasn't exactly the way the story was first told, however. It was reported by Marsh's biographer, Joseph Mills Hanson, in *The Conquest of the Missouri, being the Story of the Life and Exploits of Captain Grant Marsh* (1909) that Comanche had been on board the *Far West* with the other survivors.

Why the literary license was taken has never been explained. Was it Hanson's own dramatic creation, or a long ago recollection by Marsh that Comanche was surely on the crowded ship amidst the commotion of that night 36 years before? Or perhaps it was planned that he would go onboard, but as packed as the ship was, it was decided to spare him the stress of being cooped up for several days. One way or the other, we have no account of him being onboard by any of the men who were there.

Instead, Comanche stayed with the men of the 7th Cavalry who, after delivering the wounded to the *Far West*, marched upland with their horse and camped at the mouth of the Bighorn River, just below the Yellowstone River. Comanche was in better shape than some first thought. His wounds had been cleansed, probably with a zinc wash, and with nourishment he was able to walk from Reno's camp the 20 miles to the ship,15 miles of it without an overnight break.

Following the *Far West's* departure, he apparently walked an additional two days to the Bighorn camp, and at the end of July, another four days to the cavalry's next camp at the new Rosebud Depot, at the mouth of the Rosebud River. Dr. Stein was there, the veterinary surgeon who had stayed behind at the Powder River Depot when the cavalry moved on to the Little Bighorn valley. While he only had two days before he would leave on the next packet boat to Fort Lincoln, he gave time to extracting some of the bullets from Comanche's wounds.

Here, too, the number of wounds varied widely, from seven to well into the double digits, also with varying opinions as to whether they were all bullet wounds or some caused by arrows. Suffice to say, Stein removed a number of bullets.

The wounds, as far as we know, were all limited to the flesh, certainly concerning for the infections that can start at the sites. But there was never mention of lameness, or damage to bones or internal organs, and the resilient mustang continued to make progress as, without doubt, he enjoyed "special guest" status with the men of the 7th while waiting for his ride downriver.

The steamer, the *E.H.Durfee*, arrived at the Rosebud Depot on August 5, the next boat (another sternwheeler) after Dr. Stein's, heading for Fort Lincoln.[23] The passenger that boarded there might well have gone unnoticed save for the steamer's crew and others onboard, if not for a story filed by a reporter at the depot on August 10, that ran in the *Chicago Tribune* on August 20, 1876:

> Hardly a day passes but brings some eloquent reminder of the terrible disaster to General Custer's command. The steamer *Durfee*, which passed down the river several days since, had on board a horse, which was suffering from some severe bullet wounds received in that last charge. It was owned by Captain Keogh, 7th Cavalry, who was killed at the Battle of the Little Big Horn, and is named Comanche.
>
> When discovered it carried seven bullets, which were extracted, and it was determined to attempt to save its life. It was accordingly shipped down the river and is now comfortably quartered at Fort A. Lincoln. Today it is the only living thing to remind one of the awful carnage. Comanche is an old soldier ... and his honorable wounds should require that he be placed on the retired list with full pay.[24]

Comanche returned to Fort Lincoln on August 10, 1876. While the reporter's recommendation to retire Comanche with full pay had merit, the horse's supporters did even better by him, in short order elevating him to a command rank at the fort.

BEFORE KEOGH LEFT ON THE LITTLE BIGHORN CAMPAIGN, HE HAD asked Nelly Martin if he was killed, to bury him at Auburn, in upstate New York, and on October 25, 1877 the Martin family honored his wishes. The local newspaper, the *Auburn Morning Herald*, published an obituary that, if length and detail were any indication, brought out most of the city's some 20,000 citizens to mourn a local hero and adopted son. It was raining as the procession formed in front of the St. James Hotel at 2:00 p.m., and included among the marchers three generals and ten other officers of high rank, and representatives of the 49th New York Militia. The flag atop the State Armory was at half-mast, as were many flags around Auburn. In summary, the newspaper noted: "The obsequies were most solemn and imposing, and in every way befitting the rank and record of the fallen brave in whose honour they were held." [26]

Keogh was buried in the Martin family plot in the Fort Hill Cemetery in Auburn, and the next year a handsome, white marble monument was installed. Keogh was the only Irish-born officer at the Battle of the Little Bighorn, and his birth at Orchard, County Carlow, Ireland, was prominently noted on the front of the obelisk, as was his brevet rank of Lieutenant Colonel. The last stanza of *The Song of the Camp* by Bayard Taylor was also inscribed:

Sleep soldiers! Still in honored rest
Your truth and valor wearing:
The bravest are the tenderest, —
The loving are the daring.[27]

Andrew Alexander, husband of Nelly's sister, Evy, said of his friend: "A hero in battle, he was as tender as a woman to those he loved ...Those who had the honor of his friendship will mourn his loss as long as they live."[28]

But it was Alexander's obituary for the *Army & Navy Journal* that painted the most vibrant picture of Keogh. If it was biased, as it would be hard for a friend's words not to be, it nevertheless conveyed the spirit of the man, his strength and will, as well as anything ever written about him.

> Thousands of the gallant soldiers of Buford's Division will recollect the dashing young soldier carrying the orders of his General amid

> the smoke of battle, always gayest when in the hottest fire, always cheeriest when enduring the greatest hardships and privation. His magnificent figure and handsome face, with the color mounting at the noise of battle, always incited to gallant deeds.[29]

At one point during his years in the military, Keogh had written his brother, Tom, that he felt satisfied because in some small measure he had achieved what he wanted. The soldier of fortune who set out to fight other men's wars, had done exactly that. Nelly Martin outlived Keogh by another 50 years, and every year until she died, on March 25, the anniversary of his birthday, she remembered all he had done and what he meant to her by placing flowers on his grave.[30]

But the buckskin horse,[31] as the Indians called Comanche, had another role ahead of him. He was Captain Keogh's pride and now he would be that of the 7th Cavalry. By his very presence, the lone survivor of The Last Stand would begin to assuage people, mute their anger, and see it replaced with gratitude that this brave horse had made it through.

Chapter 9

SECOND COMMANDING OFFICER

NEWSPAPER HEADLINES BLARED IT OUT IN LARGE TYPE: MASSACRE AT the Little Bighorn. Every last man under General Custer's direct command had died, 210 soldiers killed by the Indians of the Northern Plains. The news broke during the nation's 100th anniversary celebrations, throwing a pall over festivities from coast to coast. People were stunned, frightened, and outraged. How could this happen, they wanted to know. Wasn't the Indian problem largely settled? They demanded explanations, called for an investigation and, mostly, wanted retribution. The army grabbed onto the last, taking it as a signal to step up the pressure against the Indians. Public anger was their justification to end the Indian problem once and for all.

In the long and brutal conflict with the Plains Indians, the Battle of the Little Bighorn was the Indians' greatest victory and the army's worst defeat. But for the Indians, it was a short-lived victory. Within a year, most Indians had moved onto the reservations. Sheridan, the mastermind of the ill-fated campaign of the spring of 1876, sent Terry and Crook back out that fall, their contingents bolstered with every available man they could find, their mission to scour the northern territories and kill Indians where they found them. The 7th Cavalry alone signed on 600 new recruits known as Custer's Avengers.[1] In September , the cavalry notched its first victory, destroying the Sioux encampment at Slim Buttes in the Black Hills, indiscriminately killing men, women and children, then pillaging and burning the village.[2]

Following the Little Bighorn debacle, the army moved to establish two new forts in Montana, Fort Custer in 1877 and Fort Keogh in 1878. Fort Custer was located on a high point between the Bighorn and Little Bighorn rivers and remained active until 1898. Today only a monument marks the spot. A precursor to Fort Keogh, the Tongue River Cantonment was started a month after the Battle of the Little Bighorn, northwest of the battle site where the Tongue River meets the Yellowstone River. Two years later, the fort was moved a mile to the west and renamed as Fort Keogh.[3] Unlike many forts, when their function protecting settlers ended, Fort Keogh was tapped for other uses and is still in service today.

But along with the army's tough stance, commanders soon realized that they had a powerful symbol in their corner—Comanche, the lone survivor of Little Bighorn. He had languished for two days on the battlefield, then was able to summon enough strength to walk away with his rescuers. It was a true and very powerful story, and people were captivated by it. They looked upon Comanche as heroic, noble, almost sacrosanct; a brave horse that epitomized the courage of the cavalry. People came to see him, at Fort Lincoln and at patriotic events in the area, this symbol of hope and survival against unbelievable odds. The Mustang was the cavalry's golden boy, both in color and in the image he projected. Visitors gazed at Comanche, uplifted by his presence even as they remembered what had happened, while the army continued the job at hand. They would make sure the Battle of the Little Bighorn was its last defeat in the Indian wars.

COMANCHE HAD QUIETLY SETTLED BACK INTO LIFE AT FORT LINCOLN, from the moment he arrived, the toast of the base. He was put on the sick list, his several deep wounds still in the process of healing. However, early reports that he was so grievously injured that he had to be suspended in a sling within his stall for a year before he was strong enough to walk unassisted, seem rather farfetched. This was, after all, a horse that had spent nearly six weeks in the field with the 7th Cavalry's rescue party, including several days marching between camps. If he was strong enough to do that, it is reasonable to believe that by the time he arrived at the fort, his condition had improved to the extent that he could remain upright and mobile.

Comanche was hovered over and pampered. He had any number of attendants, or so it would seem given the various names mentioned as caretakers. The pride associated with contributing to the care of Comanche spoke to his importance to everyone, much the same as did the several men who claimed to have found him on the battlefield. Once Dr. Stein resigned his post as veterinary surgeon, his request for a raise in salary having been denied, it doesn't appear that the post was filled soon. But as horsemen managed to do before and since, the men continued the necessary care themselves. Stall rest, wound care, limited and then increasing exercise, all would have been in order. Even more, the same inherently strong body and mental toughness that kept Comanche alive on the battlefield, brought him back to health at Fort Lincoln and with that, fanned the reputation that made him a lovable character on base.

YET, NO ONE COULD HAVE IMAGINED THE HEIGHT TO WHICH Comanche would rise after the death of his partner, Myles Keogh. Little more than a year and a half after he returned to Fort Abraham Lincoln, Comanche was named the Second Commanding Officer of the 7th Cavalry, and while it was clearly a ceremonial honor, it was Comanche's alone, never given before or since. General Orders No. 7 were issued by Colonel Samuel Sturgis, commander of the 7th Cavalry, still headquartered at the fort. One of his sons, Lieutenant

James Sturgis, had died with the 7th Cavalry at the Battle of the Little Bighorn, and the commander took personal interest in Comanche. The orders, issued on April 10, 1878, set down in specific and caring words a guarantee of the best care available for the revered warhorse, as a member of the 7th Cavalry for the rest of his life. They read as follows:

> (1) The horse known as 'Comanche,' being the only living representative of the bloody tragedy of the Little Big Horn, June 25th, 1876, his kind treatment and comfort shall be a matter of special pride and solicitude on the part of every member of the Seventh Cavalry to the end that his life be preserved to the utmostlimit. Wounded and scarred as he is, his very existence speaks in terms more eloquent than words, of the desperate struggle against overwhelming numbers of the hopeless conflict and the heroic manner in which all went down on that fatal day.
>
> (2) The commanding officer of Company I will see that a special and comfortable stable is fitted up for him, and he will not be ridden by any person whatsoever, under any circumstances, nor will he be put to any kind of work.
>
> (3) Hereafter, upon all occasions of ceremony of mounted regimental formation, 'Comanche,' saddled, bridled, and draped in mourning, and led by a mounted trooper of Company I, will be paraded with the regiment.
>
> By command of Col. Sturgis,
> E.A. Garlington, First Lieutenant
> and Adjutant, Seventh Cavalry.

The orders also solved a personal matter for Sturgis, whose daughter had on occasion been quietly riding Comanche to give him some exercise. Permission had been given by Henry Nowlan, now a captain and commander of Company I, having stepped into his friend, Keogh's, post. But then, as the story goes, another young woman at the fort asked Nowlan if she, too, could ride Comanche, and Sturgis' daughter registered her displeasure. Exactly why she did not want to share Comanche, we don't know. But number two of the orders solved the problem neatly; no one would ride Comanche ever again.[4]

AWARDING COMANCHE SUCH AN HONOR WAS UNIVERSALLY APPROVED. John Hay, whose career in government stretched from private secretary to President Lincoln to secretary of state to presidents William McKinley and Theodore Roosevelt, was moved to write a poem, *Miles [sic] Keogh's Horse.* In its cadence and many stanzas it recalls Tennyson's *Charge of the Light Brigade*, that young Keogh would have known 20-odd years before. In the middle stanzas, Hays describes Comanche's survival:

Alone from the field of slaughter,
Where lay three hundred slain
The horse, Comanche, wanders,
Keogh's blood upon his mane.

Of all that stood at noon-day
In the fiery scorpion ring,
Myles Keogh's horse at evening
Was the only living thing.

And Sturgis issued the order,
Which future time shall read
While the love and honor of comrades
Is the soul of the soldier's creed

He said, "Let the horse, Comanche,
Henceforth till he shall die,
Be kindly cherished and cared for
By the Seventh Cavalry.[5]

The news of his promotion to Second Commanding Officer gave Comanche even more publicity, including a creative piece for the Bismarck *Tribune* of May, 10, 1878, in which a reporter purported to interview the horse himself at Fort Lincoln. As retold, the interviewer "asked the usual questions," which Comanche "acknowledged with a toss of his head, a stamp of his foot and a flourish of his beautiful tail." Soon enough, the reporter let an attendant answer the questions, including a retelling of how Comanche was found on the Little Bighorn battlefield, the extent of his wounds and aftercare, and an appealing description of him then: "Comanche is not a great horse, physically talking; he is of medium size, neatly put up, but quite noble looking. He is very gentle. His color is 'claybank.' He would make a handsome carriage horse."[6]

What he would have thought about the last suggestion, one can only wonder. But the public continued to be enamored of Comanche, and even a pretend interview with the famous horse would have delighted his many fans.

BEYOND THE OFFICIAL MANDATES OF GENERAL ORDERS NO. 7, THERE were a host of daily do's and don'ts, and while they may not have carried the same weight as Sturgis' declarations, they were viewed with utmost seriousness. Comanche's diet, for one, was to continue the same as what Keogh had given him, a special blend of oats and hay. It went without saying that fresh water should always be available in his drinking trough. The horse was still to have daily exercise, perhaps trotting him, riderless, alongside a horse and rider. It was to be in the early part of the morning, before the sun got too hot, and would be followed by a rubdown. In late afternoon, he was to be rubbed down again before he ate dinner.[7]

Comanche reciprocated with his best indulged behavior. Now officially retired, he was at liberty on base, free to amble the grounds wherever he wished. Clearly the "Lord of the Manor," he could be merciless when it came to front lawns and gardens, leaving notice of his visits whenever and wherever Nature called. Sunflowers, purposefully grown to attract bees and birds, were a favored snack of Comanche's, who probably thought they were really grown for him. For things he couldn't take for himself, he had others well trained. The women on base shared fresh-baked biscuits and cookies, officers brought sugar cubes from their club, and children, especially, produced treats whenever the horse wanted them—and let it be said, no one minded.

The women, clearly a part of Comanche's support system, also devised some entertainment for themselves and their favorite horse, teaching him to play kickball and fetch, things Keogh could likely never have imagined. It is said, they would take Comanche out to the parade ground and toss balls to him, that he would retrieve in his mouth and bring back to the thrower. He also apparently became adept at kickball, managing to return the ball with a kick of his front feet when it came his way.[8]

COMANCHE'S LOVE OF HENNESSEY-LACED BRAN MASHES REMAINED A constant, becoming a frequent offering from his caretakers. Whether they were a pleasant tonic against any residual pain as his body mended itself, or just because Comanche liked the taste of brandy, is anyone's guess. But his love of liquor increased with time, mostly for the buckets of beer hung on the door of the enlisted men's canteen, a treat from the men on payday and, no doubt, other times.

People's affection for Comanche was grounded at Fort Lincoln, and the role he occupied, as everyone's favorite member of the cavalry, was serious beyond what was spelled out in General Orders No. 7. Even when he pushed through fresh-hung laundry, strewing pieces on the ground to the dismay of housewives, or otherwise caused a ruckus, his behavior was considered to be beyond reproach. Anyone who dared to reprimand him was seen as out of line. An epithet hissed between clenched teeth might not be noticed, but anything approaching physical discipline of the Second Commanding Officer was subject to court martial. Nor did it ever come up, not even as a whispered rumor.

For all the indulgences of his good life, there was one request made of Comanche. On June 25 each year, it was his official duty to perform as the caparisoned horse, led riderless by an officer walking beside him, in the parade that memorialized the Battle of the Little Bighorn. He was draped in black cloth, saddled and bridled, with a pair of spurred boots placed backwards in the stirrups of the empty saddle. His presence, dressed as he was, symbolized that the deceased had fallen as a warrior and would ride no more.[9] But in a larger sense, as many looked at Comanche and remembered Keogh, the horse's appearance year after year served to remind people of the many brave men who gave their lives at the Little Bighorn, and of the extraordinary sacrifice they made in the country's efforts against the Indians.

Such pomp was part of cavalry life, and it was in their blood, even Comanche's. Beyond the solemnity of the June 25 parade, the strains of *Garryowen* coming from the parade ground on any given day were a summoning call, often bringing him at a trot to join the column. Company I would be falling in for a drill, and Comanche would take his place at the head of the line, just as if Keogh was astride his back. Did he remember the myriad times he had done this with the captain, the firm feel of his long legs on his sides? In his mind, did he hear the deep brogue say softly, "Good boy," after the drill was finished and the colors retired? Fanciful thoughts, indeed. But why not, when one considers the long run that Comanche and Keogh had together?

HE HAD BEEN OWNED BY AN IRISHMAN (IN TIME, PROUDLY American), and one might think Comanche had picked up a little of the Irish proverbial luck. He had lost Keogh, but soon after he returned to Fort Lincoln, Comanche found a new friend who would fill the void that the death of the captain had created. His name was Gustave Korn, a member of Keogh's Company I and, by virtue of an unexpected parting from the company, he had survived the Battle of the Little Bighorn.

Like Keogh, Korn was an immigrant, arriving in the U.S. from Silesia, in Central Europe, in 1852. He enlisted in the 7th Cavalry in 1873, and served as Keogh's orderly, as he was doing in the last moments when Company I regained the ridge, following the separation with Reno's battalion. Like most enlisted men, Korn was riding a horse from the pack, and typical of many of these mounts, Korn's horse could be tough to ride. He was remembered, variously, as being skittish and hard-mouthed, and that day, with Korn on his back, the horse decided to put both vices into motion. Korn had dismounted to tighten the girth as the rest of the column moved forward, but as quickly as Korn was back in the saddle, the horse took off, grabbing the bit, locking his jaw, and rushing past the other men. From then, Korn and his horse were out of control as they tore away from Keogh's column, galloped through the Indian camp, arrows striking the horse as they went, and finally raced up a bluff to where Reno was establishing a defensive position. Pulling up, Korn dismounted as his horse, spent from wounds and utter exhaustion, collapsed and died, having saved Korn's life.

Immediately, Korn turned to tending the wounded among Reno's men, joining several others who repeatedly braved Indian fire to bring water from the river for those pleading for it. One of Reno's officers questioned Korn as to why he left his company, but it was clear from his answer that he had had no intention to avoid the battle. Any further question of wrong doing was dismissed and he went on to have a long, exemplary career, with praise for his performance entered into his official record at each reenlistment.[10]

Korn went back out with Terry's column, riding with him through the fall as they searched for Indians, and upon returning to Fort Lincoln was named the fort's official blacksmith.[11] As Keogh's orderly, he had known Comanche, so pitching in to care for him was perfectly understandable. The connection that grew was described as deeper and, as it turned out, twice as long, as that with Keogh. Comanche, they said, followed Korn around like a puppy dog.[12] At the same time that Sturgis issued General Orders No. 7, he made Korn Comanche's official caretaker.[13]

IN 1879, THE PUBLIC'S CLAMOR FOR AN INVESTIGATION INTO WHAT happened at the Battle of the Little Bighorn was finally answered when a U.S. Army Court of Inquiry was convened in Chicago. The inquiry had been called at Reno's request, after he had endured repeated insinuations and outright criticism for his actions during the battle, namely that he was drunk and retreated too quickly, and his actions caused the destruction of his battalion.[14] Reno's conduct was scrutinized during the inquiry, but the court exonerated him of wrong doing.

Nonetheless, the investigation produced enough blame to go around, most of it leveled against Custer and starting from the very top with Ulysses Grant. Writing in *The Army & Navy Journal*, Grant said: "I regard Custer's massacre as a sacrifice of troops, brought on by himself, that was wholly unnecessary...," adding that he should have met Terry and Gibbon on June 26, rather than pushing on and being forced to confront the Indians alone on June 25.[15]

Sheridan also faulted Custer for dividing his troops. "Had the 7th

Cavalry been kept together, it is my belief it would have been able to handle the Indians at the Little Bighorn and under any circumstances it could have at least defended itself...," he said, pointing out that separated into three detachments, the Indians with their overwhelming numbers had a huge advantage.[16]

Custer had his supporters, as well, most certainly led by his widow, Libbie, who fiercely protected her husband's reputation for the rest of her long life. Elizabeth Bacon Custer lived to 91 years old, dying in 1933, by which time most of General Custer's antagonists were already deceased. But well over a century after the Battle of the Little Bighorn, historians and others are still debating the circumstances that played out and brought about the devastating outcome on June 25, 1876; military, historians, and private citizens still arguing about who was right and who was wrong.

In 1879, the 7th Cavalry transferred to Fort Meade, South Dakota, a fort that had been established the year prior to protect new settlements in the northern regions of the Black Hills. Sturgis took command of the new fort in July, and Comanche took up residence in August. Nine years later, in 1888, the 7th Cavalry returned to Fort Riley where, 22 years before, the regiment had first been organized. It was there that the long-established schedule of two creatures of habit, Comanche and Korn, was occasionally upset, producing a story that was a favorite of the men who knew them.

Late in the afternoon, Korn always showed up at Comanche's stall to brush him, give him dinner, and settled him in for the night. But at times he was otherwise engaged, and when he didn't show up as expected, Comanche went looking. First he would go hunting around the base, but if that casual search didn't produce Korn, the horse seemed to know exactly what to do next. He would head down the Junction City road, about five miles into town, to a specific house where Korn's lady friend lived. It is said Comanche would bang on the door with his hoof, and when Korn opened the door, stick his head inside,[17] effectively ending Korn's visit, and getting his buddy back.

COMANCHE AND GUSTAVE KORN HUNG OUT TOGETHER, THE BEST OF friends for almost 15 years. But in the end, Comanche lost him, too. In December 1890, several companies of the 7th Cavalry were ordered to the Pine Ridge reservation in South Dakota, among them Company I, still commanded by Captain Nowlan. Comanche at age 28 was still fit enough to join the pack horses that went along.

The plan was to defuse what was perceived to be the growing influence of the Ghost Dancers, a movement that preached the rebirth of the Indians' world before the white man came to destroy it. Their leader was the aging Chief Sitting Bull, whose vision had accurately predicted the debacle at the Battle of the Little Bighorn. What worried the army was the Ghost Dancers could be doing a war dance, which would herald an Indian uprising .

The cavalry's move onto the reservation was conceived as proactive; their target the village led by Big Foot near Wounded Knee Creek, where they would disarm the Ghost Dancers. By then, most Indians had moved to the reservations, but this band was among a few that still resisted the change. Tensions were high, exacerbated by the shooting death of Sitting Bull in mid-December. The cavalry, admittedly jittery, trained guns on the village and then proceeded to round up the Indians and take their weapons. Suddenly, a shot rang out, from which side never determined but, on December 28, it set off an explosion of violence that overwhelmed the village.

In what some characterized as retribution for the Battle of the Little Bighorn, this time far more Indians were killed than soldiers, an outcome that was the polar opposite of that other battle 15 years before. The number of Indians who died, including many women and children along with the men, ranged from 150 to 300, and reflected those who were killed during the battle and more who succumbed to their wounds thereafter. The Battle of Wounded Knee effectively destroyed the threat of the Ghost Dancers and, finally, the Sioux Nation.

The cavalry lost 31 men, among them Gustave Korn. Comanche did not see him die, and in the days that followed his return to Fort Riley with the rest of the pack horses, he waited for Korn to show up at his stall. When he didn't, Comanche began roaming around the base looking for his friend, but unlike other times, the outcome was disappointing.

Another farrier, Samuel Winchester, stepped up to befriend and care for Comanche, but neither he nor the horse's many other friends, though they tried their best to bolster their horse's spirits, could stop his slow decline. They could see him losing his taste for simple pleasures. He no longer rooted through garbage pails; the buckets of beer he used to guzzle with relish, now seemed to leave him more morose than before he drank them. He lay around for hours at a time, in his stall or outside in a mud wallow.

By summer, it was clear that Comanche was slipping away. Four years prior the army had transferred ownership of the horse to Nowlan, thus removing him from the army's payroll.[18] Whatever the reason, perhaps purely economic, it somehow seemed fitting to give him to Keogh's best friend. But, still emotionally Comanche was the regiment's horse, and Nowlan gathered some of the officers together to discuss the inevitable. When the time came, what would they do with their much-loved horse? They could not bear the finality of a burial with nothing beyond. With that, the idea of preserving him took hold. The naturalist, Lewis Lindsey Dyche, was interested and offered his services.

Comanche died not long after midnight on November 7, 1891,

age 29, after suffering through the day with colic. He had never recovered from the loss of his friend, Korn, the life force and energy that had defined him, even as he aged, ebbing away. Winchester spent the final day with him, at the end cradling Comanche's head in his lap as the old warhorse passed on. Then he penned this note, remembering:

> Fort Riley, Kansas, Nov. 7th, 1891 — In memory of the old veteran horse who died at 1:30 o'clock with the colic in his stall while I had my hand on his pulse and looking him in the eye — this night long to be remembered.[19]

At first light that morning, a telegraph was sent to Professor Dyche of the Natural History Museum on the University of Kansas campus in Lawrence. It was the summons he expected, and he had packed a bag with everything he would need. That same morning he took the train to Junction City.

Chapter 10

HERO FOR THE AGES

Lewis Dyche made the one hundred mile trip from Lawrence to Junction City, Kansas on Saturday, November 7, 1891, arriving at Fort Riley after midnight, 24 hours after Comanche had died. Working through that night, all of Sunday and into the second night, he harvested what was needed to begin to preserve the great horse. Crated to take back with him, Dyche took the hide, the skull, and the major bones. The work to recreate Comanche would be done at the professor's taxidermy laboratory at the University of Kansas, and the preservation had to begin as quickly as possible.

The cavalry had chosen Dyche because of his well established reputation as a naturalist and taxidermist. During the year, as the Professor of Anatomy and Physiology, Taxidermist and Curator of Mammals, Birds and Fishes, he taught at the University of Kansas.[1] Summers he spent in the field, hunting animals as he had since he was young, adding them to a burgeoning collection of preserved specimens from North America and the Arctic. But despite the many animals that he had worked on, none carried the celebrity and emotional attachment to the public as did Comanche.

The agreed upon price for Dyche's work was $400. However,

when the project was completed and he presented his bill to the 7th Cavalry, the money didn't materialize, and the professor readily made them an amended offer. In lieu of pay, he would be happy to keep Comanche, first exhibit him at the upcoming World Exposition in Chicago, and then give him a permanent home at the university. The army was clearly pleased, some might say relieved at Dyche's second suggestion. The 7th Cavalry considered itself an organization that could (and did) move on short notice, and to bring along the soon-to-be large, preserved Comanche would be problematic. More crassly, too, now that the Indian troubles were virtually ended, there wasn't the public relations use for him anymore. As well, once Nowlan took ownership, it would have been difficult to get the Army to pay the taxidermy fee for one, officially at least, no longer theirs. So, on all counts, giving Comanche to Dyche was the perfect solution.

Befitting his stature, the 7th Cavalry buried Comanche's remains at Fort Riley with full military honors. At the time, he was the first horse so honored. While we don't know the particulars, we can be sure that it was a most solemn and important event on base, attended by many including military and dignitaries coming from elsewhere. In all probability, Comanche's flag-draped casket rode on a horse-drawn caisson. It would have been accompanied by a military escort, including a caparisoned horse, the role Comanche assumed in so many memorial parades. Then, at the burial site, there would have been a rifle salute, music by a military band and, lastly, a bugler playing *Taps* as his body was lowered into the ground, all of it entirely fitting for the great horse.

Since Comanche's burial, history records one other horse was buried with full military honors. That was Black Jack, the black Morgan-Quarter Horse cross that marched as the caparisoned horse in more than 1,000 Armed Forces funerals, most of them at Arlington National Cemetery. A few other famed horses, notably Chief, the last cavalry horse on the army payroll, and Sergeant Reckless, the U.S. Marines' warhorse in the Korean War, have been buried with honors.

Whether their burials included all the prescribed elements of a funeral with "full" military honors is debated, but they were, nonetheless, cherished members of the military buried with reverence and dignity.

BACK AT HIS LABORATORY IN LAWRENCE, KANSAS, PROFESSOR DYCHE began utilizing the skills he was noted for. He had been trained by the world renowned taxidermist, William T. Hornaday, Dyche having spent a summer working with Hornaday when the latter was chief taxidermist at the National Museum in Washington, D.C. Using what was known as the Hornaday Method, Dyche soaked the hide in a pickling solution, then in a solution with arsenic. The skeleton was rebuilt with a variety of materials including wood, metal, string, wire, nails, excelsior, newspaper, and plaster of paris. All of that was covered, then sculpted out of a medium known as creek-bank clay and, finally, the hide was stretched over the entire model.[2] The result was the ultimate in taxidermy in its time, a real-life vision of Comanche that would draw crowds to admire their famous horse.

As Dyche worked with Comanche, he was finally able to put to rest the guesswork and describe exactly what wounds the horse suffered at the Battle of the Little Bighorn. There were seven in all, by his assessment three of them were severe and four were flesh wounds. The three that were severe he pinpointed as one in the neck behind the left shoulder, the bullet having passed clear through; a second was in the front part of the neck; the third was in the flank, the result of another bullet that passed clear through, this one exiting between the hind legs.[3]

It took two years of exacting, painstaking work, but when it was completed, Comanche went to Chicago, his restored self a toast of the World's Columbian Exposition of 1893. The huge fair was being held to commemorate the arrival of Christopher Columbus in the New World 400 years before, as well as to tell the world that Chicago had come back, risen from the fire that had destroyed much of the city 22 years ago. The buildings were mostly white, thus the exposition's name as The White City, and its scale and grandeur were staggering, as were the number of spectators —more than 27 million—who attended during its six months run.

States, countries, and territories all had buildings that showed off their specialties and achievements, and in the Kansas Pavilion that was the work of Lewis Dyche. One-third of the building was devoted to a new type of display idiom, a monumental diorama called the *Panorama of North American Mammals*. In size and diversity, it was an extraordinary collection of stuffed and mounted animals, realistically posed in a natural setting. Every one of them had been captured and preserved by Dyche and his assistants through taxidermy, including bison, grizzly bears, mountain lions, elk, mountain goats, prairie dogs, and moose.[4]

Nearby, in his own space, the meticulously preserved Comanche was drawing thousands of spectators to take their first look at the famous horse. His presence, next to a collection of wild animals, was an acceptable style of the time, a mix of the scientific with things that were sentimental and historic. All of it celebrated the exposition's themes of accomplishments, particularly the ideas of expansion and conquest of the continent and, from that, the victory of civilization over savagery.[5] Comanche, survivor of the Battle of the Little Bighorn, fit right in—and the public loved him.

Both the panorama and Comanche's area were open, with no glass wall between the visitors and the displays. The wild animals in their tableau setting, and Comanche standing quietly by himself, could be accessed by any intrepid visitor, if only to pet a furry nose or stroke a neck or, in Comanche's case, take a few tail hairs as a souvenir. Dyche, to protect his exhibit from vandalism and theft, built living quarters for himself within a papier mâché mountain at the back of the panorama, which he was able to access by moving a boulder in the mountain.[6]

The World's Columbian Exposition stayed open for six months, from May 1 to October 31, 1893, after which Dyche took Comanche back to the University of Kansas, his home from then on.

At the university, Comanche first lived at Snow Hall,[7] then the natural history building, again sharing space with the myriad wild animals. From the time of his arrival, it is said that he resided just inside the main door, and much like his stay in Chicago, with nothing between him and his admirers. But unlike those days, Dyche had resumed teaching classes and working in his laboratory, and was not around to protect Comanche. So many of his tail hairs were pulled out —students thought they were a good luck charm—that at least twice his tail had to be replaced.

In 1901, the state legislature allocated funds to build a permanent museum at the University of Kansas for Dyche's collection of mounted specimens. Two years later, an imposing neo-Romanesque structure was completed, a tour de force of architectural details beginning with an imposing tower and arched main entrance. After Dyche's death in 1915, the building was named Dyche Hall.[8] Then, only 31 years from when it opened, the building was condemned as being structurally unsound when inspections revealed that the weak construction of the floors and ceilings could collapse, destroying Dyche's priceless collection.[9] The building was closed and the artifacts stored. Comanche spent the next nine years by himself in an auditorium basement on campus.

In 1941, Dyche Hall reopened and Comanche was back, somewhat the worse for his time in damp quarters—but still very much there. He resumed his place as a visible member of the university community, greeted fondly by those on campus as "the old boy." At exam time, just like before, students rubbed his nose or pulled out a few tail hairs for good luck. But now, back on display, it was clear to all that real the culprit was Kansan humidity, which can swing wildly from a drenching 100 percent in the spring and summer to a dry 25 percent in the winter. Despite the fact that Comanche had been preserved by one of the best taxidermists of his time, himself trained by a man at the top of the profession, nobody then understood the importance of climate control. Thus, through the seasons, Comanche's legs swelled up and shrank, parts within him rusted, and some materials broke down completely and turned to dust, and as they settled, changing the shape of his body.[10]

It was a sad sight and as it continued for years, staff at the Natural History Museum were at a loss to know just how to address Comanche's many physical problems. But even if repairs were not yet forthcoming, the public loved their horse. No longer the main-floor greeter, Comanche now resided on an upper floor of the museum, and still they came.

IN 1970, COMANCHE TOOK ON A NEW ROLE. HE HAD BEEN A warhorse by profession, then after his last battle, the best public relations representative the army had, and now the venerable "old boy" became a unifier. It happened rather unexpectedly, when American Indian students took exception to the wording of Comanche's history on a sign that was posted at his stall. The sign had been displayed for ages, a fairly typical description of what had happened in 1876; that Custer and all his men had been killed by Indians and only Comanche survived. As far as anyone could remember, no one had ever complained about what was written.

But in 1970, almost a half a century ago, the students objected to some of the language in the sign. In essence, they pointed out, Comanche was not the sole survivor, nor was the Battle of the Little Bighorn a massacre but, instead, a battle in which many Indians also survived. They wanted the suggestion, as in the old stereotype of the

Indians as savages, erased. Further, the idea that the Indians were in the wrong, and Custer and his men, massacred, were in the right, had to be changed. At the Indian students' request, the exhibit was closed. Yet, with their respect for horses as an integral part of Indian life, they never blamed Comanche.[11]

Over the next year, a committee met, listened and discussed, and eventually came up with exhibit signage that was acceptable to both sides. In essence, Comanche was presented as a symbol of the conflict between the U.S. Army and the Great Plains Indians; the Battle of the Little Bighorn was described as an Indian victory; and the Battle of Wounded Knee was changed to read, the Massacre of Wounded Knee.[12] With new, reworded signage installed, Comanche's exhibit reopened. Both sides said that they had learned, expanded their views, and come to a resolution that pleased everyone—and they agreed that Comanche had brought them together.

HIS FANS KEPT COMING, BUT BY THE 80S, ANYONE COULD SEE THAT Comanche's body was in terrible shape, but nothing was being done. Then, a calamitous accident in the overnight hours changed the debate from "What can we do?" to "How soon can we do it?" Comanche, survivor of the Indian wars, was almost drowned by cascading water from an upstairs sink that overflowed, flooding the five floors below and soaking the horse. The blame (as such) was pinned on a large African bird that, as it was thawing, slipped into a sink and hit the faucet, managing to both start the waterfall and plug the drain. The next day, March 6, 1986, Tom Swearingen, then exhibits director at the museum, faced the inevitable. Ninety-five years after Dyche had begun preserving Comanche, Swearingen was going to have to restore him to his former self.[13]

Besides the sodden horse that the deluge had wrought, when the director began addressing the effects of time and atmosphere, he was aghast. As he started to look inside, gingerly opening up seams in

Comanche's hide, Swearingen saw how bad the damage really was. Still, persevering when he sometimes felt like running away, and often calling on his personal mantra of "Don't panic,"[14] Swearingen brought Comanche back. Techniques had improved, of course, as had materials, and for the first time the renewed horse went to live in a climate-controlled glass stall, the inside weather always at 60 percent humidity.

YET, AS GOOD AS COMANCHE LOOKED AFTER SWEARINGEN RESTORED him, new methods led to newer methods, and in 2005 the horse was ready to be reinvigorated once again. This time, he was also moved, down to his former home on the main floor, a space more inviting to visitors. Not unlike the challenges of restoring him, moving Comanche took thought, time, and detailed planning, including construction of a foam board model, a rolling platform, and a ramp, and the work of an expert team that then exhibits director, Bruce Scherting, led through dry runs before the big day.[15]

Once he was moved from the fifth floor to his new location, Comanche was ready for his restoration, the assignment going to Terry Brown, a museum restorer from Loretto, Minnesota. Despite a short time frame between other projects, the chance to work on Comanche was an offer Brown couldn't refuse; working 110 to 125 hours a week, he completed Comanche's restoration in five weeks. Knowing how much people like to watch the work in progress, at Brown's suggestion, the university built a temporary glass-walled studio in which he restored the horse. People came to watch all day long, some of them knocking on the door to ask questions.[16]

THAT COMANCHE IS STILL AT THE UNIVERSITY OF KANSAS SAYS MUCH about the grit and resolve of everyone from past chancellors to the students. Over time, other organizations mounted forceful, sometimes strident campaigns, insisting that the horse, for myriad reasons, rightfully belonged with them. Fort Riley, having sent Comanche away so long ago, wanted him back to where he had lived in the last years of his life; the Little Bighorn Battlefield felt he clearly belonged in their museum, the battlefield being the place where his singular story began. The university administration, alumni, and the student body would have none of it. At one point the then chancellor, replying to the army's efforts to take him back, said that Comanche is

> quite unconcerned and calm about the hullabaloo which has been blowing about his ears. He seems to want to stay right where he is very much indeed and I am confident that he will remain there.[14]

Later, when the argument was with the people at the Little Bighorn battlefield, a newspaper published letters supposedly written by Comanche, in which he said he preferred the Kansas climate over that of Montana.[18] The students even petitioned the university to make sure he didn't leave.

Today, his color is golden, his eyes are clear, and he looks robust standing in his new, state-of-the-art, climate controlled case. What the chancellor said then holds true today. Comanche likes it at Dyche Hall, and he's staying.

He is part of the university, in more than 125 years visited by many hundreds of thousands of people from all over the world, still today coming to stare, to marvel, and to pay respects to the famous Comanche.

EPILOGUE

My father first told me about Comanche when I was about eight years old. I don't remember how it came up, exactly; maybe we were reading a book together, or had just come home from a Wild West movie. Dad would have seen an opening to tell me this short, simple story of a horse that survived an Indian battle. Though not by profession, he was the consummate educator, and I know he loved adding little bits of information to whatever we were doing, to create more interest for me.

So, there it was, a childhood memory that stayed alive. When I revisited it as an adult, a few years ago, I found an intriguing, complex story—of a horse and rider whose legacy grew beyond anything that was apparent in their lives. In a sense, it's a backwards story. Comanche became famous and then people came to know Myles Keogh.

Most people don't know much about Keogh, perhaps only that he was a cavalryman who fought for us, in the Civil and Indian wars. But this Irishman stood for hundreds of thousands of immigrants who chose to fight in our wars, at times they made up almost half of our fighting force. Though they never forgot their homelands, many of them went on to stay and build their lives here.

Keogh never knew a fort had been named for him. He died the year before. Most of the forts from those times have since disappeared, some quite literally. Others, whatever parts survived, were saved as historic relics to remind people of what had come before. Fort Keogh, however, is still going! Its original function as a center from which to fight Indians and protect settlers is long over. So, too, the remount station that it next became, from which more horses went to the battlefields of Europe in World War I than from any other remount station. After that, in 1924, the fort went to the U.S. Department of Agriculture, and continues today as the Fort Keogh Livestock and Range Research Laboratory, tackling the problems of range management and animal husbandry as they come and go.

As to Comanche, he was one of those good horses that we horsemen covet when they come our way. Tough and unflappable as he was, he couldn't save Keogh's life. But in surviving himself, he gave them both a place in history. If he hadn't clung to life, we would know nothing of the determined Captain Myles Keogh and the resilient Comanche, and I think we are the richer for knowing them.

ACKNOWLEDGMENTS

Thank you, Angele McGrady, my wonderful editor and lifelong friend. I could not have done this without you. Your sure hand in helping me shape the story made a good one so much better.

Thank you, Joseph Brockbank, my proofreader. No matter how many times I went over copy, you would see things missed. Even so, you were enjoying the story, and I appreciated your reviews.

Thank you, Dominick Bosco, my talented designer, for giving me exactly the cover and book I wanted. You understood right away what I was looking for in a cover, and then came back with much more.

Thank you, Jean McWilliams, owner of Taborton Equine Books, for your friendship and support, and for your generosity in launching this book.

Thank you, Terry Brown, for allowing me to use the photos of you and Comanche. They bring him alive. Thank you, too, to the University of Kansas for the photo of "the old boy" today--still looking fine.

And to my husband, Walter, who has lived with Comanche and Myles Keogh a long time, thank you for putting up with them and me, and always for your support and kindness.

ABOUT THIS BOOK

Dominick Bosco, the designer of this book and its cover, wears several hats. Besides designing books, he is a bestselling author and website designer. Formerly, he was also senior editor at Prevention Magazine. With his wife Stacy Jenel Smith, he is the owner of Story Hill Creative and Story Hill Books.

He chose the traditional font, Times New Roman, for the text of this book, and formatted it using Vellum. The main cover font is Arbutus.

Contact: db@storyhillcreative.com

This book was printed by Phoenix Press using electricity generated by wind. The company's Northwind 100 turbine, located on site in New Haven, Connecticut, harnesses coastal winds ranging from a low of six miles per hour to a high of 55 miles per hour, to produce power that enables the plant to operate with clean, renewable energy.

NOTES

Chapter 1: SETTING COURSE

1. U.S. Government, *Application for Citizenship*, 1869.
2. Elisabeth Kimber and Robert Doyble, *A Visit to Orchard House*, 2008, www.littlebighorn.info/ 4.
3. Kimber, 5.
4. *Keogh (No. 2) of Leinster*, Library Ireland, 2005, www.libraryireland.com/ 4.
5. John Ryan, *History and Antiquities of the County of Carlow*, 1833. www.askaboutireland.ie/ 2.
6. Kimber, 9.
7. Thomas Bartlett, *The 1798 Irish Rebellion,* www.bbc.co.uk/ 5.
8. Kimber, 7.
9. Ibid.
10. *Keogh (No. 2),* 3.
11. John P. Langellier et al, *Myles Keogh—The Life and Legend of an "Irish Dragoon" in the Seventh Cavalry,* 1991, 50.
12. Ibid., 51.
13. *Irish Potato Famine,* The History Place, www.historyplace.com/ 2000.
14. Ibid.
15. Ibid.
16. Langellier, 50.
17. Kimber, 6.
18. Myles Kavanaugh, *The Village Schoolmaster—John Conwill (1802-1880),* www.igp-web.com/ 4.
19. Kimber, 7.
20. *Ulster History Circle/Charles Lever (1806-1872),* Hidden Gems and Forgotten People, 2007, www.hidden-gems.eu/ 1.
21. Alfred, Lord Tennyson, *The Charge of the Light Brigade,* selected stanzas.
22. Kimber, 8.

Chapter 2: THE POPE CALLS

1. *The Widow's Mite—Private Relief During the Great Famine,* History Ireland, www.historyireland.com/2018, 7.
2. *The Irish in Italy,* The New York Times archives, 6/21/1860, www.nytimes.com/ 4.
3. Oliver O'Hanlon, *The Irishmen who fought for the pope,* Irish Times, www.irishtimes.com/2014, 1.
4. Nir Arielli, *The Foreign Enlistment Act,* The International History Review, vol. 38, 2016, issue 4, abstract.
5. *History of Carlow,* Irish Genealogy Projects, www.igp-web.com/ 1.
6. Des Ryan, *The Pope's Emigrants,* www.limerickcity.ie/pdf, winter edition, 2003, 2.
7. Kimber, *Orchard House,* 8.
8. *The Wild Geese History,* The Wild Geese, www.thewildgeese.irish/2018, 2.
9. Ibid.
10. Robert Doyle, *A Brief Conflict, Part 3 of 3 of 'The Pope's Irish Battalion',* The Wild Geese, www.thewildgeese.irish/2011, 2.
11. Ibid.

12. Robert Doyle, *The Pope's Irish Battalion, 1860,* www.historyireland.com/vol. 18, Sept/Oct 2010, 1.
13. Doyle, *A Brief Conflict,* 3.
14. Doyle, *Pope's Battalion, 1860,* 2-3.
15. Doyle, *Irish Battalion,* part 2, 2.
16. Ibid., part 1, 3.
17. Doyle, *Pope's Battalion, 1860,* 3.
18. Ibid.
19. Patrick Keyes O'Clery, *The Making of Italy, 1856-187,* www.books.google.com/ 207.
20. Ibid.
21. Doyle, *Pope's Battalion,* part 2, 2.
22. O'Clery, 215.
23. Ibid., 217.
24. Doyle, *Pope's Battalion, 1860,* 3.
25. Ibid.
26. O'Clery, 209.
27. Ryan, *Pope's Emigrants,* 21.
28. Ibid.
29. Doyle, *Irish Battalion,* part 3, 2.
30. Doyle, *Pope's Battalion, 1860,* 3.
31. William Henry Flayhart III, *The Inman Steamship Company Limited, 1850-1886,* The Northern Mariner, No. 4, 2002, 32.
32. C.R Vernon Gibbs, *British Passenger Liners of the Five Oceans from 1838 to the Present* 1863, 217.
33. Java Saxena, *Castle Garden: Where Immigrants Came Before Ellis Island,* www.behindthescenes.nyhistory.org/2013, 2.
34. Asa Greene, *A Glance At New York,* www.ephemeralnewyork.wordpress.com/2019, 4.
35. Ibid.

Chapter 3: THE UNION CAUSE

1. *B&O Railroad Station, New Jersey Avenue and C Street NW,* www.civilwarwashingtondc1861-1865.blogspot.com/2011/10/ 1.
2. Kenneth Winkle, *Washington: Capital of the Union.* www.essentialcivilwarcurriculum.com/ 3.
3. *History & Culture—Civil War Defenses of Washington,* www.nps.gov/cwdw/2019, 1.
4. *The Metropolitan, aka Brown's Marble Hotel,* www.streetsofwashington.com/2009/ 1.
5. Ibid.
6. Ibid., 2.
7. Ibid., 4.
8. Langellier, *Life and Legend,* 63.
9. Robert Doyle, *the Pope's Irish Soldiers and the Civil War,* www.irishamericancivilwar.com/2010/11/09/blog entry.
10. Charles L. Convis, *The Honor of Arms—A Biography of Myles W. Keogh.* Westernlore Press, 1990, 15.
11. Christopher Hibbert, *Garibaldi: Hero of Italian Unification,* St. Martin's Griffin, 2008, 330-332.
12. *Shaping a Volunteer Army,* American Battlefield Trust, www.battlefields.org/2018, 1.

13. *James Shields,* www.bioguide.congress.gov/2019, 1.
14. *Battle of Port Republic—Shenandoah at War,* www.shenandoahatwar.org/2018, 2.
15. *Shields,* 1.
16. Langellier, 70.
17. Ibid., 69.
18. Brian C. Pohanka, *The Irish Knight,* www.custer.over-blog.com/2000, 3.
19. Ibid.
20. *Shields,* 1.
21. Convis, 22.
22. *Preamble to the U.S. Declaration of Independence*, 7/4/1776.
23. *The U.S. Civil War 1861-1865,* History Place, Timeline, www.historyplace.com/1996, 1.
24. Ibid., 2.
25. *Port Republic,* 2.
26. Ian Kenneally, *Courage and Conflict—Forgotten Stories of the Irish at War*. Cork, Ire.: Collins Press, 2009, 1.
27. Ibid.
28. Langellier, 35.
29. Damian Shiels, *Remembering the many Irish lost at Gettysburg,* www.irishexaminer.com/7/3/2013, 1.
30. Langellier, 30.
31. *Timeline,* 3.
32. *Halleck takes command of the Union army,* Day in History, www.history.com/2009, 1.
33. *Timeline,* 3.
34. *George B. McClellan,* American Battlefield Trust, www.battlefields.org/2018, 2-3.
35. Ibid.
36. *Lincoln Issues Emancipation Proclamation*, History, www.history.com/2018, 1.
37. Ibid., 2.
38. *Timeline,* 3.
39. *McClellan,* 2.
40. *Irish Knight,* 3.
41. *The Military Staff,* www.battlefields.org/2018, 2.
42. Ron Soodalter, *Buford Hold the High Ground.* www.opinionator.blogs.nytimes.com/2013/06/29/ 4.
43. Ibid., 2.
44. *Battle of Fredericksburg,* History, www.history.com/2018, 1.
45. *Joseph Hooker,* American Battlefield Trust, www.battlefields.org/2019, 1.
46. *Timeline,* 4.
47. J.Heiser, *Cavalry Battles&Leaders,* Gettysburg Nat Park, 1998,www.civilwar.com/ 1.
48. Soodalter, 3.
49. *Brandy Station,* American Battlefield Trust, www.battlefields.org/2018, 3.
50. J.D. Petruzzi, *Six Weeks in the Saddle with Brig. Gen. John Buford,* 2005, 1.
51. *Brandy Station,* 3.
52. Convis, 31.
53. Soodalter, 4.
54. Petruzzi, 3.
55. Ibid.

56. *General John Buford's Report on his Cavalry's Action at Gettysburg* (summary excpt),1.
57. *John Heiser,* 12/12/2018.
58. Convis, 31.
59. Petruzzi, 3.
60. Langellier, 78.
61. Ibid.
62. Ibid.
63. Ibid.
64. Convis, 33.
65. *John Buford,* American Battlefield Trust, www.battlefields.org/2018, 2.

Chapter 4: CARRYING ON

1. *George Stoneman, Jr.,* www.militarymuseum.org/2018, 1.
2. Ibid., 3.
3. *Giesboro Point Cavalry Depot—Civil Was Rx,* www.civilwarrx.blogspot.com/2016/04/ 3.
4. *Civil War Cabins,* U.S. Army Heritage & Education Center, www.ahec.armywarcollege.edu/ 2-3.
5. Ibid., 3.
6. Ibid., 4.
7. Langellier, *Life and Legend,* 79.
8. Winkle, *Capital of the Union,* 4.
9. Ibid.
10. Ibid., 5.
11. Ibid., 4.
12. Langellier, 79.
13. Ibid.
14. Ibid.
15. Ibid.
16. Ibid., 80.
17. Ibid., 81.
18. Ibid.
19. Convis, *Honor of Arms,* 40.
20. Trevor Steinbach, *History lesson—Union & Confederate horse doctors of the Civil War,* Herald Chronicle, 9/21/2017, www.heraldchronicle.com/ 1.
21. Ibid.
22. Chris Wilkinson, *Civil War Prisons,* New Georgia Encyclopedia, www.georgiaencyclopedia.org/2014, 1.
23. *Old Charleston City Jail—Charleston, South Carolina,* www.atlasobscura.com/2018, 1.
24. Langellier, 81.
25. *Andersonville Prison,* American Battlefield Trust, www.battlefields.org/ 1.
26. Ibid., 2.
27. Langellier, 81.
28. Ibid.
29. Langellier, 82.
30. Ibid.
31. Ibid.

32. *Timeline*, History Place, 6.
33. *Appomattox Court House,* History, www.history.com/ 2.
34. A.W. Trelease, *Stoneman's Raid,* Encyclopedia of North Carolina, www.ncpedia.org/2006
35. Langellier, 83.
36. Ibid., 84.
37. Ibid.
38. Ibid.
39. Ibid.
40. Mark L. Bradley, *The Army and Reconstruction, 1865-1877,* U.S. Army Center of Military History, 2015, 15.
41. Ibid., 26.
42. Ibid., 72.

Chapter 5: SECURING THE FRONTIER

1. K.Weiser, *Kansas Cowtowns,* Legends of America, www.legendsofamerica.com/2018, 1.
2. *Railroads in Kansas,* Kansapedia, Kansas Historical Society, www.kshs.org/ 1-3.
3. Convis, *Honor of Arms,* 50.
4. Ibid., 43.
5. Ibid., 50.
6. Ibid., 42.
7. *George Stoneman, Jr.,* 1.
8. *John Buford,* American Battlefield Trust, www.battlefields.org/ 1.
9. *Little Bighorn Battlefield,* National Park Service, 16.
10. Brian C. Pohanka, *'Born a Soldier':Myles Walter Keogh,* Part 1,www.thewildgeese.irish/ 2.
11. *History of Fort Riley,* www.home.army.mil/riley/ 1.
12. Ibid., 3.
13. K. Weiser, *Fort Wallace,Kansas,* Legends of America, www.legendsofamerica.com/2018
14. *Life at Fort Wallace,* Fort Wallace Memorial Association, www.ftwallace.com/ 1-2.
15. R. Douglas Hurt, *The Construction and Development of Fort Wallace, Kansas, 1865-1882,* www.kshs.org/ 1.
16. Ibid., 2.
17. *History of Fort Riley,* www.home.army.mil/ 1.
18. Hurt, 2.
19. Convis, 53.
20. Hurt, 2.
21. Langellier, 85.
22. Ibid., 86.
23. Ibid., 84.
24. Ibid.
25. Ibid.
26. Pohanka, *The Irish Knight,* 5.
27. Ibid., 8.
28. Langellier, 110.
29. Convis, 97.
30. Doyle, *The Irish at the Little Bighorn,* 2.
31. Langellier, 128.

32. Ibid.
33. Convis, 97.
34. Langellier, 129.
35. Ibid.
36. Pohanka, *Knight,* 6.
37. Robert Doyle, *Custer's Last Irishman: The Irish Who Fought at the Battle of Little Bighorn, Part 5*, www.thewildgeese.irish/ 2.
38. Convis, 97.
39. *Legend of Garryowen,* U.S. First Cavalry website.

Chapter 6: A PARTNERSHIP BEGINS

1. *United States Army Remount Service,* 1-2.
2. *Cost of a cavalry horse,* www.in2013dollars.com
3. Convis, *Honor of Arms,* 63.
4. Ibid.
5. *Lt. Col. Alfred H. Sully,* www.nps.gov/ 1.
6. Convis, 62-63.
7. Ibid.
8. *Evolution of Military Veterinary Medicine,* U.S. Army Medical Department, Office of Medical History, www.history.amedd.army.mil/2009, 2.
9. Raymond L. Welty, *Supplying The Frontier Military Posts,* Kansas Historical Quarterly, May 1938, vol. 7, no. 2, www.khsh.org/ 154.
10. Karen Jones, *The story of Comanche: horsepower, heroism and the conquest of the American West,* Journal of War & Society, vol. 36, issue 3, 2017, www.tandfoline.com/8.
11. S.C. Gwynne, *Empire of the Summer Moon—Quanah Parker and the Rise and Fall of the Comanches,* NY, NY: Schribner, 2010, 29.
12. Ulysses S. Grant, *The Complete Personal Memoirs of Ulysses S. Grant*, 1885.
13. Phillip Aston Rollins, *The Cowboy: His Characteristics, His Equipment, and His Part in the Development of the West,* p. 42-43.
14. *Custer's Last Standard Bearer,* 5.
15. Erin Lodes, *Hammurabi and Hippocrates: Veterinary Medicine BCE,* College of Veterinary Medicine, Michigan State University, 1-3.
16. Ibid.
17. Ibid.
18. Ibid.
19. *Evolution of Military Veterinary Medicine,* U.S. Army Medical Dept., 1.
20. Langellier, *Life and Legend,* 120.
21. Kathy Weiser, *Fort Abraham Lincoln, North Dakota,* Legends of America, www.legendsofamerica.com/2018, 1.
22. Irvin Haas, *Citadels Ramparts & Stockades—America's Historic Forts,* NY, NY: Everett House, 1979, 37.
23. Convis, 92.

Chapter 7: THE LAST STAND

1. Peter Cozzens, *Ulysses S. Grant Launched an Illegal War Against the Plains Indians, Then Lied About It.* www.smithsonianmag.com/ 1.
2. Haas, *Citadels,* 37.

3. *1874 Custer Expedition to the Black Hills,* 1.
4. Cozzens, 1.
5. Ibid., 5.
6. Kenneally, *Courage,* 191.
7. John A. Doerner, *The Boys of '76,* True West, www.truewestmagazine.com/ 2.
8. Jones, 8.
9. John S. Gray, *Veterinary Service on Custer's Last Campaign.* The Kansas Historical Quarterly, Vol. 12, Autumn 1977, Number 3, www.kshs.org/ 253.
10. Ibid., 254.
11. Jones, *Comanche,* 9.
12. Pohanka, *Knight,* 8.
13. Convis, *Honor of Arms,* 107.
14. Jones, 13.
15. Convis, 120.
16. Robert M. Utley, *The Indian Frontier—of the American West 1846-1890.* Albuquerque, NM: University of New Mexico Press, 1984.
17. National Park Service, *Battle of the Little Bighorn Handbook,* 3.
18. John S. Gray, 256.
19. Convis, 111-113.
20. Langellier, 133.
21. Ibid, 134.
22. NPS, *Battle,* 4.
23. Ibid, 5.
24. Convis, 147.
25. Ibid, 146.
26. Thomas Powers, *How the Battle of Little Bighorn Was Won.* Smithsonian Magazine, November 2010. www.smithsonianmag.com/ 11.7
27. Langellier, 140-141.
28. Convis, 158.

Chapter 8: ENDING AND BEGINNING

1. *Custer Battlefield Handbook,* National Park Service, Historical Handbook, Custer Battlefield, 6.
2. *1879 U.S. Court of Inquiry.*
3. *Custer Handbook,* 9.
4. Convis, *Honor of Arms,* 159.
5. Ibid., 145.
6. Ibid.
7. Thomas Powers, *How the Battle of the Little Bighorn was Won*, 20.
8. Ibid., 20.
9. Edward Luce, *Custer Battlefield,* ebook, Loc. 216.
10. Evan Connell, *Son of the Morning Star,* NY, NY: Promontory Press, 1993, 291.
11. Convis, 154-155.
12. Ibid., 165.
13. Powers, 22.

14. Nathaniel Philbrick, *The Last Stand—Custer, Sitting Bull, and the Battle of the Little Bighorn.* NY, NY: Penguin Books, 2010, 279.
15. *U.S. Court of Inquiry.*
16. *Custer Battlefield,* 11.
17. Daniella Hanna, *Grant Marsh—Nautical Hero of the Plains,* North Dakota Horizons, www.ndhorizons.com/ 3-4.
18. NPS Handbook, 13.
19. Luce, Loc. 216.
20. Col. W.A. Graham, *How Helena Scooped Bozeman,* The Custer Myth: A Source Book of Custerania, 1953, 2-3.
21. Ibid.
22. *Custer Battlefield,* 15.
23. John S. Gray, 261.
24. Ibid., 262
25. Ibid
26. Pohanka, *Knight,* 9.
27. Langellier, *Life and Legend,* 160-161.
28. Pohanka, *Irish Knight*, 8
29. Ibid.
30. Convis, 181.
31. John Monahan, *Myles W. Keogh,* Carloviana—Journal of the Old Carlow Society,1958, 10.

Chapter 9: SECOND COMMANDING OFFICER

1. Convis, *Honor of Arms,* 156.
2. *The Battle of Slim Buttes—1876,* History and Culture, www.nativepartnership.org/ 1.
3. Kathy Weiser, *Fort Keogh, Montana,* Legends of America, www.legendsofamerica.com/ 2018, 1.
4. Gordon Baker, *Comanche's Ride to Destiny,* ebook, Loc. 165.
5. Convis, 173-175.
6. John S. Gray, *Veterinary Service,* 263-264.
7. Baker, Loc. 188, 196.
8. Ibid.
9. *The Caparisoned Horse,* Arlington National Cemetery, www.arlingtoncemetery.net/ 1-2.
10. Winkler Albert. *The Case for a Custer Battalion Survivor: Private Gustave Korn's Story* BYU Scholars Archive, Brigham Young University, 2013. www.scholarsarchive.byu.edu/ 47.
11. Ibid.
12. Convis, 173.
13. Ibid., 132.
14. Ibid., 166.
15. Convis, 165.
16. Ibid., 173.
17. Ibid., 75.
18. Ibid., 176.

Chapter 10: HERO FOR THE AGES

1. John H. McCool, *Finger in the Dyche/KUHistory, www.*kuhistory.ku.edu/ 1.
2. Dickie Wooten, *Share a Piece of History—Comanche, Warhorse.* Breakthrough Magazine, Issue 52, Summer, 1998, 36.
3. Barron Brown, *Comanche—The U.S. Army Horse Who Survived the Battle of the Little Big Horn.* Kansas City, MO: Burton Publishing Company, 1935. Kindle version, Uncommon Valor Press; 2015, Loc. 249.
4. William B. Ashworth, Jr. *Scientist of the Day—Lewis Lindsay Dyche.* Linda Hall Library, 3/20/2019. www.lindahall.org/ 2.
5. Langellier, *Life and Legend,* 24-25
6. Ashworth, 2.
7. McCool, 2.
8. Ibid., 2-3
9. Ibid.,2.
10. Wooten, 36, 52.
11. Langellier, *Life and Legend,* 27.
12. Ibid.
13. Wooten, 37.
14. Ibid., 38.
15. Terry Rombeck, *Comanche Called to New Post.* www.ljworld.com/2005/may/07/ 1-2.
16. *Conversation with Terry Brown,* 6/15/2019.
17. Langellier, 28.
18. Ibid., 26.

PHOTOGRAPHS

1) Public domain. **2)** Geograph.org.uk—1816353.jpg; © sarah777. **3), 4)** National Archives. **5), 6)** Library of Congress. **7), 8)** Public domain. **9)** Little Bighorn Battlefield National Monument. **10), 11)** Library of Congress. **12)** Montana Historical Society, public domain. **13)** Public domain. **14), 15)**Library of Congress. **16), 17), 18)** Terry Brown/President—Museum Professionals, Inc., Restoration Artist/Diorama Artist, www.museumprofessionals.com, terry@museumprofessionals.com **19)** University of Kansas Natural History Museum/Jason Daily Photography.

BIBLIOGRAPHY

BOOKS

Baker, Gordon. *Comanche's Ride to Destiny with the U.S. Seventh Cavalry.* 1962. Kindle.

Bradley, Mark L. *The Army and Reconstruction, 1865*—1877, Washington, D.C.: U.S. Army Center of Military History, 2015.

Brown, Barron. *Comanche—The U.S. Army Horse Who Survived the Battle of the Little Big Horn.* Kansas City, MO: Burton Publishing Co., 1935. Kindle: Uncommon Valor Press, 2015.

Brown, Dee. *Bury My Heart at Wounded Knee—An Indian History of the American West.* NY, NY: Henry Holt and Co., 1970.

Convis, Charles L. *The Honor of Arms—A Biography of Myles W. Keogh.* Tucson, AZ: Westernlore Press, 1990.

Connell, Evan S. *Son of the Morning Star—Custer & The Little Bighorn.* NY, NY: Farrar, Straus & Giroux, 1984.

Donovan, James. *A Terrible Glory—Custer and the Little Bighorn.* NY, NY: Little, Brown and Co., 2008.

Gibbs, C. R. Vernon. *British Passenger Liners of the Five Oceans—A Record of the British Passenger Lines and their Liners, 1838 to the Present..* London: Putnam & Co., Ltd, 1963.

Gwynne, S. C. *Empire of the Summer Moon—Quanah Parker and the Rise and Fall of the Comanches.* NY, NY: Scribner, 2010.

Haas, Irvin. *Citadels Ramparts & Stockades—America's Historic Forts.* NY, NY: Everest House, 1979.

Kenneally, Ian. *Courage and Conflict—Forgotten Stories of the Irish at War.* Cork, Ire.: Collins Press, 2009.

Langellier, John P.; Cox, Kurt Hamilon; and Pohanka, Brian C., eds. *Myles Keogh—The Life and Legend of an "Irish Dragoon" in the 7th Cavalry.* El Segundo, CA: Upton and Sons, 1991.

Lawrence, Elizabeth A. *His Very Silence Speaks, Comanche—The Horse Who Survived Custer's Last Stand.* Detroit, MI: Wayne State University Press, 1989.

Luce, Edward S. *Keogh, Comanche and Custer.* St. Louis, MO: John S. Swift Co., 1939.

Luce, Edward S. and Evelyn S. *Custer Battlefield—National Monument, Montana.* Washington, D.C.: National Park Service, U.S. Dept. of the Interior, 1961. Kindle.

Michno, Gregory F. *Lakota Noon—The Indian Narrative of Custer's Defeat.* Missoula, MT: Mountain Press Publishing Co., 1997.

Mulligan, Fergus. *Captain Myles Keogh, the 7th Cavalry and the battle of the Little Big Horn, 140 years ago.* Monograph, 12/19/2016. www.publishing.ie/pdf.

O'Clery, Patrick Keyes. *The Making of Italy 1856-187.* Paternoster House, Charing Cross Road, London: Kegan Paul, Trench, Trübner & Co., Ltd., 1892. www.books.google.com/

Philbrick, Nathaniel. *The Last Stand—Custer, Sitting Bull, and the Battle of the Little Bighorn.* NY, NY: Penguin Books, 2010.

Powers, Thomas. *The Killing of Crazy Horse.* NY, NY: Random House, 2010.

Utley, Robert M. *The Indian Frontier—of the American West 1846-1890.* Albuquerque, NM: University of New Mexico Press, 1984.

ARTICLES

Andersonville Prison/American Battlefield Trust. www.battlefields.org/2018.

Ashworth, William B., Jr. *Scientist of the Day—Lewis Lindsay Dyche.* Linda Hall Library, 3/20/2019. www.lindahall.org/

Bartlett, Thomas, *The 1798 Irish Rebellion.* www.bbc.co.uk/history/british/2018.

The Battle of the Little Bighorn—Comanche, Possible Survivors. Wyoming Tales and Trails. www.wyomingtalesandtrails.com/2018.

The Caparisoned Horse. Arlington National Cemetery. arlingtoncemetery.net/017.

Black Hills—Stories of the Sacred. Indigenous Religious Traditions. www.sites.coloradocollege.edu/2019.

Castle Garden—Experiences of an English Emigrant. The New York Times Marine Intelligence Column—December 23, 1866. Posted to TheShipsList by Paul Petersen, 25 Nov 1997. www.members.tripod.com/2018.

*Catholic Encyclopedia (1913)/Louis- Christophe-Leon-Juchault de la Moriciè*re.www.en.wikisource.org/2018.

Cochran, Diane. *Historic horse on display in Kansas.* The Billings Gazette, 6/23/2005. www.billingsgazette.com/2016.

Cosgrove, Neil F. *Myles Keogh, A True Hero Hidden in Myth,* 4.9.2010. www.praoh.org/2016.

Cozzens, Peter. *Ulysses S. Grant Launched an Illegal War Against the Plains Indians, Then Lied About It.* www.smithsonianmag.com/2019.

Doyle, Robert. *Custer's Last Irishmen: The Irish Who Fought at the Battle of the Little Bighorn, Parts 1-5.* www.thewildgeese.irish/2019.

_______. *The pope's Irish battalion, 1860.* www.historyireland.com/vol. 18, Sept/Oct, 2010.

Flayhart, William Henry, III. *The Inman Steamship Company Limited: Innovation and Competition on the North Atlantic, 1850-1886.* The Northern Mariner, vol. 12, No. 4, 29-46. www.cnrsscm.org/northern_mariner/2002.

Greene, Asa. *A Glance at New York.* c. 1850. www.ephemeralnewyork.wordpress.com/ 2019.

Gray, John S. *Veterinary Service on Custer's Last Campaign.* The Kansas Historical Quarterly, Volume 43, Autumn 1977, Number 3. www.kshs.org/

Hanna, Daniella. *Grant Marsh—Nautical Hero of the Plains.* North Dakota Horizons, #58, 2016. www.ndhorizons.com/

Harvey, Douglas. *Custer's Last Standard Bearer.* Dept. of History, University of Kansas, 11.7.1891. www.kuhistory.com/

History of Fort Riley. www.home.army.mil/riley/2019.

Hurt, R. Douglas. *The Construction and Development of Fort Wallace, Kansas, 1865-1882.* Kansas Historical Society, Spring 1977, vol. 43, no. 1. www.kshs.org/2019.

The Irish in Italy. New York Times archives, 6/21/1860. www.nytimes.com/1860/06/21/archives/

Irish Potato Famine. The History Place, 2000. www.historyplace.com/2018.

Jones, Karen. *The story of Comanche: horsepower, heroism and the conquest of the American West.* Journal of War & Society, Vol. 36, Issue 3, 2017; published online 02 Aug 2017 www.tandfonline.com/

Kavanagh, Myles. *The Village Schoolmaster—John Conwill (1802-1880).* Carlow County—Ireland Genealogical Projects. www.igp-web.com/

Kimber, Elisabeth and Doyle, Robert. *A Visit to Orchard House, Leighlinbridge, County Carlow. 2008.* www.littlebighorn.info/pdf.

Krishtalka, Leonard. *KU's Comanche a symbol of historic shift.* LJWorld.com. www.ljworld.com/news/2005/nov/19/

Keogh (No. 2) Of Leinster. Library Ireland. www.libraryireland.com/Pedigrees1/keogh-2-heremon.php, 2017.

McCool, John H. *Finger in the Dyche/KU History.* www.kuhistory.ku.edu/2019.

McNally, Frank. *An Irishman's Diary.* The Irish Times, 10.3.2008. www.irishtimes.com/opnion/2017.

National Park Service. *Little Bighorn Battlefield.* Historical Handbook: Custer Battlefield www.nps.gov/2017.

Nye, Colonel Elwood. *Marching with Custer: A Day to Day Evaluation of the Uses, Abuses and Conditions of the Horses on the ill-fated Expedition of 1876.* Army Medical Bulletin, The Long Riders Guild Academic Foundation, 1941. www.lrgaf.org/

O'Hanlon, Oliver. *The Irishmen who fought for the pope.* The Irish Times. www.irishtimes.com/2018.

Pohanka, Brian C. *The Irish Knight—Myles W. Keogh's Life and Times.*

www.custer.over-blog.com/2016.

The pope's Irish battalion, 1860. History Ireland, Vol. 18, Issue 5, Sept/Oct 2010. www.historyireland.com

Powers, Thomas. *How the Battle of Little Bighorn Was Won.* Smithsonian Magazine, November 2010. www.smithsonianmag.com/

Battle of the Little Bighorn. Little Bighorn Battlefield National Monument.

www.nps.gov/2016.

Rombeck, Terry. *Comanche Called to New Post.* www.ljworld.com/news/2005/may/07/

Ryan, Des. *The Pope's Emigrants.* The Old Limerick Journal, Winter Edition 2003.

www.limerickcity.ie/

Rydell, Robert W. *World's Columbian Exposition.* Encyclopedia of Chicago. www.encyclopedia.chicagohistory.org/2019.

Showalter, Dennis. *Wild Irish Geese/History Net.* www.historynet.com/2018.

Soodalter, Ron. *Buford Hold the High Ground.* www.opinionator.blogs.nytimes.com/2013/06/29/

Steinbach,Trevor. *History lesson—Union & Confederate horse doctors of the Civil War*

Herald Chronicle, 9.21.2017. www.heraldchronicle.com/

A Terrible Glory by James Donovan. Book Review, Perspectives of the Past.

www.perspectivesofthepast.com/2017.

Winkle, Kenneth J. *Washington: Capital of the Union.* Essential Civil War Curriculum. www.essentialcivilwarcurriculum.com/2019.

Winkler Albert. *The Case for a Custer Battalion Survivor: Private Gustave Korn's Story*

BYU Scholars Archive, Brigham Young University, 2013. www.scholarsarchive.byu.edu/

Wooten, Dickie. *Share a Piece of History—Comanche, Warhorse.* Breakthrough Magazine, Issue 52, Summer, 1998.

INDEX

If you liked *Comanche And His Captain…*

They Called Her Reckless

A True Story of War, Love And One Extraordinary Horse

Set against the history of the Korean War, often called the Forgotten War, this unusual and inspiring story of a small Korean pony and her fellow Marines speaks to an incredible human-horse connection and the power it unleashed. Acquired to haul the heavy shells uphill to the 75mm recoilless rifles, Reckless served alongside her buddies for two years in the war zone, packing more ammunition than anyone thought possible, saving lives, raising spirits, and winning the love and respect of all who knew her.

"A lifelong horsewoman, Barrett writes with an instinctive understanding for these complex animals that were an integral part of war for many centuries ... And having immersed herself in the role of Marines in the Korean War, she also has acquired an understanding for that special breed as well. ... A moving tale about a unique bonding of horse and human." — *Semper Fi* Magazine